how you'll do
EVERYTHING
based on your
ZODIAC
SIGN

created by

CHRISSY STOCKTON

THOUGHT CATALOG
Books

THOUGHTCATALOG.COM
NEW YORK · LOS ANGELES

Published by Thought Catalog Books, an imprint of the digital magazine Thought Catalog, which is owned and operated by The Thought & Expression Company LLC, an independent media organization based in Brooklyn, New York and Los Angeles, California.

This book was produced by Chris Lavergne and Noelle Beams. Art direction and design by KJ Parish. Illustrations by Ava Puckett. Special thanks to Chrissy Stockton and Bianca Sparacino for creative editorial direction and Isidoros Karamitopoulos for circulation management.

Visit us on the web at thoughtcatalog.com and shopcatalog.com.

Made in the United States of America.

ISBN 978-1-949759-26-6

Zodiac Signs Reference Guide

♈ ♉ ♊ ♋ ♌ ♍ ♎ ♏ ♐ ♑ ♒ ♓

ARIES DATES:
March 21 – April 19

TAURUS DATES:
April 20 – May 20

GEMINI DATES:
May 21 – June 20

CANCER DATES:
June 21 – July 22

LEO DATES:
July 23 – August 22

VIRGO DATES:
August 23 – September 22

LIBRA DATES:
September 23 – October 22

SCORPIO DATES:
October 23 – November 21

SAGITTARIUS DATES:
November 22 – December 21

CAPRICORN DATES:
December 22 – January 19

AQUARIUS DATES:
January 20 – February 18

PISCES DATES:
February 19 – March 20

Table of Contents

Here's What Kind Of Crazy Ex You Are

BASED ON YOUR ZODIAC SIGN

ARIES

Aries are the kind of crazy exes who become increasingly reckless after a breakup. Their personal loss has them feeling sluggish, but instead of laying on the couch watching *Sex and the City* reruns and binge-eating burritos like a normal person, they crave exciting distractions to distance themselves from their negative emotions. If one of your exes has suddenly bought a motorcycle, started experimenting with new drugs, or developed an interest in bouldering, they are likely an Aries.

TAURUS

Tauruses are the kind of crazy exes you never hear from again but who make broad sweeping changes in their lives afterwards. They cut out mutual friends without saying goodbye and punish their next potential partner by making them jump through a hundred hoops before they'll commit or open up. Once they've been hurt, they're tempted to close down and not give anyone the opportunity to hurt them again.

GEMINI

Geminis are the kind of crazy exes who make important life decisions based on feeling shitty about themselves post-breakup. They'll cut off all their hair or move to a new country or decide that now is the right time to quit their day job to pursue their art full-time. The thing Geminis are best at is passion, so when they feel sad they want to combat it by getting excited about something new. If you've ever had someone totally change personalities after breaking up (think from dad bod to gym bro), they're probably a Gemini.

CANCER

Cancers are the kind of crazy exes who become extremely slutty (but only toward their ex). They miss the person they loved. They're hurt and they want to: a) recapture the good feelings they used to have; and: b) show their ex what they are missing with someone who can love them as deeply as Cancers can. So they end up having a lot of very confusing breakup sex (which in their minds is makeup sex). If you have an ex that became hypersexual after you rejected them, they are likely a Cancer.

LEO

Leos are the kind of crazy exes who start posting everything cool they do on social media in an effort to convince everyone around them that they're sooooo much better off. They miss the attention and affection they got from their relationship, and they need to fill that void somehow. Leos know they're posting too much (and kind of needy, tbh), but they can't help themselves.

VIRGO

Virgos are the kind of crazy exes who will methodically figure out how to ruin your life (and probably do it). They have all the skills they need: intelligence, focus, problem-solving—and a nasty breakup gives them the single-minded desire. Because they're so very Virgo, you won't even know they're crazy exes. One day your life will just fall apart and you won't know someone was the mastermind behind the whole thing.

LIBRA

Libras are the kind of crazy exes who go out of their way to win over your mutual friends. When you started the relationship, you may not have had any mutual friends, but when you leave it, rest assured that your friends will forever probably like Libra better. Libras are amazing at dealing with people, and their favorite way to say "fuck you" is to make the people *you* like love *them* more.

SCORPIO

Scorpios are the kind of crazy exes who get straight-up aggressive about you leaving them. They'll leave 'wtf' comments on your social media and trash you to mutual friends. In their minds, *no one* hurts Scorpio, so they have to fight (what they perceive as) fire with fire.

SAGITTARIUS

Sagittariuses are the kind of crazy exes who never mention the breakup ever again, like complete psychos. Sagittarians pride themselves on not being overly emotional; they don't brood over broken relationships for long. To others, this seems bizarre to the point of disordered, but it's an earnest expression of their personality to cut ties and move on in a practical fashion.

CAPRICORN

Capricorns are the kind of crazy exes who will try to make you feel guilty for moving on. They'll invent reasons to keep you in their life—you owe $7.22 from your share of the electricity bill, you RSVP-ed to a cousin's wedding as their plus-one, you left half a box of tea behind at their apartment—and then they'll use their in-person time to guilt you into reconciling with them. More than any other type, Capricorns are prone to on-again/off-again relationships. They can drop their cold exterior and pretend to be chill and fun-loving long enough to lure someone back, but it always ends up the same.

AQUARIUS

Aquariuses are the kind of crazy exes who find someone else to take care of and become obsessed with their new pet project. Aquarians can't stand to be without an interest that consumes them. They are masters of the rebound relationship. If you have an ex that met someone literally five minutes after your breakup and you can't figure out why they even like this new person, they're an Aquarius.

PISCES

Pisces are the kind of crazy exes who make you their muse. You'll read about yourself in their stories or see bits of your personality in their artwork. Creative Pisces channel all their feelings into their craft, and breaking up is no different. If you've had an ex write an about you on the internet, they're probably a Pisces.

This Is What Your Ex Still Misses About You

BASED ON YOUR ZODIAC SIGN

ARIES

Say what you will about Aries, but they're out there doing cooler shit than you. Break up with one, and you'll find yourself in bed watching *Friends* for the thousandth time while you scroll through an Insta feed of them having dinner with friends you haven't seen before in a new city on a cool boat—just about everything that makes you feel like a homebody blob without them. Aries will bring excitement to a relationship; after their relationships end, it's inevitable that their exes realize their lives are a little bit boring now.

TAURUS

No one will ever make you feel as secure as Tauruses will. They're a tough nut to crack, but once you're in, you're in for life. They don't change their minds easily, so you know that even if you're fighting at the moment or you did something to upset them, they aren't going to withdraw. The next person you date will be more volatile than this (everyone is), and you'll miss the way Taurus made it known that temporary setbacks are just that.

GEMINI

The experience of dating Geminis makes everyone else seem boring and lackluster by comparison. Geminis *ooze* passion. They wake up every day with the *joie de vivre* to do something new and exciting. It's hard to let someone who brightens up your life this much walk away.

CANCER

No one will love you like Cancers will love you. It's almost impossible not to look back for the rest of your life and wonder if your current partner loves you as deeply and as unconditionally as your Cancerian ex did. There will always be a twinge of regret there, that despite all the reasons you weren't working out, that was still the realest love you will ever experience.

LEO

Leos are leaders, but they also care very deeply about what their partner thinks of them. They will forge a unique life with anyone—always checking in, always making sure their partner is completely happy, too. After the breakup, their ex will miss how much importance Leo placed on their opinion. It's a daily ego boost that's definitely not common with most other people.

VIRGO

Virgos makes their partners' lives so, so, *so* much better than they were before. Being with one means being with someone who knows how to do *everything* and is hell-bent on upgrading your life. They'll put all your bills on auto-pay, set up your cable, and rearrange your furniture so everything just *flows*. Losing them is like flying first-class and then having to go back to coach.

LIBRA

Libras are incredibly charming and gifted, with the best social skills in the zodiac. Date one and you'll feel like you are this special partner to someone who makes you feel cool and totally understood and like there's no other couple that could be so perfect for each other. This is exactly the insecurity you'll walk away with, too. Will anyone else ever understand you so completely? Will they feel like a partner who is almost an effortless extension of yourself? Probably not.

SCORPIO

Scorpios are the perfect balance between bad bitches that can get anything done and deep lovers with high emotional intelligence. It's rare for both these things to exist in the same person, and it's likely that when your ex inevitably settles for one or the other, they miss the spark of your dual nature.

SAGITTARIUS

Sagittariuses will make staying at home and cooking spaghetti together the most fun night of your life. They have an infectious spirit and a killer sense of humor. After breaking up with one, it's hard for their ex not to miss how much *fun* they were capable of making everything. Suddenly everyone else in the world seems like they have a stick up their butt because they take everything much more seriously.

CAPRICORN

Capricorns refuse to be part of any couple that is not a power couple. From afar, they're the kind of people everyone wants to be: successful, chic, basically flawless in every way. Moving on from Capricorn is always a downgrade because you're always moving on to something lesser. You'll always wonder if your life would be bigger than it is now if you had stayed with them.

AQUARIUS

When Aquariuses date, they're on a mission to make their partner a better person. "She makes me a better person" is a trope you hear in tons of wedding vows, but in the case of Aquarius it's true. You'll start recycling because of Aquarius, you'll be less cynical—you'll be a person who discovers they are patient and feel *happy* when they get to do something nice for someone else. Moving on, you'll wonder if that was the best you'll ever be.

PISCES

Pisces are gifted artists and deep thinkers in a way that never feels phony. They are often dumped because their partner is intimidated and feels inferior. But even when they move on they will always think about Pisces and miss what it was like to be close to someone who was so special. They'll worry they took the safe road and wonder if their life would be less boring if they'd chosen differently.

The Nastiest Thing You Are Willing To Do In Bed

BASED ON YOUR ZODIAC SIGN

ARIES

Aries are known for their love of adventure and willingness to try new things. So in bed, pretty much everything is on the menu. The only deal-breaker for Aries is monotony. If you want to be a dead fish or do the same thing over and over, find a different partner.

TAURUS

Tauruses will do a lot of freaky things in bed, but they have to be the one to suggest it. Good luck getting them to try something if it was your idea first. The only hard-and-fast rule they have is they have to feel like they're in charge.

GEMINI

Oh, man. What WON'T Geminis do? Geminis are passionate and playful lovers who are always game to explore something new. They're so upbeat and positive that they'll only draw the line at anything too serious or aggressive (non-lite BDSM).

CANCER

More loving and caring than any other sign, there's not much Cancers won't do for the right partner—but they'll never be the one to suggest it. They're focused on making their partner happy, so they'll be genuinely aroused by what arouses *you* as long as you have an emotional connection with them first.

LEO

Leos will absolutely, without a doubt make the best sex partner you've ever had. Their love of being the center of attention makes them natural exhibitionists. They love showing themselves off and getting steamy attention from their partner in the process. Knowing lustful thoughts are being directed their way all day and all night is truly the Leo dream.

VIRGO

Virgos are not adventurous lovers. If you're looking to experiment, you won't be happy here. However, let it be known that they *more* than make up for it by being very, very good at what they are willing to do. Like everything else in Virgo's life, they've done a lot of Google searching and figured out how to approach perfection.

LIBRA

Libras have such exceptional people skills, they've never had to work hard for attention or affection. Chances are, they've been praised for all their vanilla sex acts, so they haven't really had an urge to explore beyond those. They'll go down on you, but they won't kiss you afterward, and that's about as spicy as it gets.

SCORPIO

Scorpios can be the best sex in the zodiac if the Scorpio you're with has learned to turn their ego down far enough to be physically open with you. They're they perfect combination of both sensual and aggressive in a push-you-against-the-wall-and-have-their-way-with-you kind of way. What's off the table? Trying to dominate them.

SAGITTARIUS

Sagittarians are almost always into butt stuff. It will inevitably start off as a joke, but somewhere along the line it became a genuine interest. If you're with Sagittarius, be warned.

CAPRICORN

Capricorns are the real prudes of the zodiac. It's not that they won't *try* anything, but they will do it in a perfunctory way so that they can brag about it later. The only real way to get them to let loose is to drop hints about how good your ex was (terrible advice in general, but desperate times...), and their competitiveness will kick in and suddenly they'll looooove to do things they turned their nose at before.

AQUARIUS

Aquarians will not do any sex act they don't consider truly evolved. Forget about domination and submission with an Aquarian, but stick around because they do care immensely about their partner's pleasure. They always return the favor.

PISCES

Pisces are creative souls who color outside the lines in bed. They are sometimes simple in their sensuality, preferring acts that emphasize emotional connection, but they will always add their own flair to otherwise ordinary acts. While not adventurous to an extreme, they happen to be the best kissers in the zodiac.

Here's How You'll Become Rich

BASED ON YOUR ZODIAC SIGN

ARIES

You'll take a risk no one else will. Aries can be incredible (or terrible) investors, gamblers, and entrepreneurs because their adventurous nature allows them to have alpha energy and take a leap when no one else will. You'll make a well-deserved fortune by betting on something everyone else is scared of.

TAURUS

Your laser focus will allow you to do something no one else could pull off. Taureans are fiercely independent—they don't need other people around for company or to approve of them. This frees up their time and energy to devote it fanatically to the projects of their choosing. When they decide to do something, the decision is over, and Tauruses will see it through until it's completed to their high standards. When Tauruses get rich, you know that they've really *earned* it because whatever happened, it was a project they pushed through with their own blood and sweat (but not tears, because…they're a Taurus).

GEMINI

You'll (finally) turn one of your passions into a wildly successful business. If there's one thing Geminis have no shortage of, it's ideas. Every day they have fifteen different ideas about how they'd like to spend their time, and they're just as passionate about every one of them. Somewhere in there is an idea that's gold; all it takes is enough focus to get the right people to pay attention to you.

CANCER

This is a tough one, because of all the signs, Cancers really don't care about money. They like money because they understand that it represents love for some people. A boss won't tell you she loves you, but she'll pay you an amount that lets you know you are valued without question. So either they become addicted to their jobs and rise through the ranks because they come to love the objective affection money has to offer, or they do the very un-feminist but very *Cancerian* thing of being the world's best support system to their partner—allowing their loved one to rake it in big time.

LEO

You'll leverage your ability to entertain people. Leos love to be the star of the show, which means they've grown up learning what entertains people. This is a rare and valuable skill. Whether it's through writing, performing, or just knowing how to create advertisements that people pay attention to, your thirst for attention will be end up being a lucrative attribute.

VIRGO

You're so damn put-together that it's almost impossible for you *not* to figure out how to make a lot of money. Virgos are insanely good at most jobs other people think are too boring to consider—which is great for Virgos because these jobs' "undesirability" or difficulty means they pay well. One person's trash is another person's treasure.

LIBRA

You'll turn your ability to get people to trust you into a valuable business partnership. That, or one of your friends will win the lottery and shower you with money because they love you so much. Libras have a mesmerizing ability to make people love them, and it's not in the fake salesperson way; they're literally just very, very good at building relationships. One day they'll make that connection with the right ($$$) person.

SCORPIO

Scorpios are confident to the point of aggression. They could sell anyone on anything, so their fortune will be made convincing other people to see things their way. Whether it's wooing investors or making a career as a salesperson, marketer, or lawyer, Scorpios have the luxury of having many paths to success because their personality is so likely to dominate them all. You'll likely make your money the old-fashioned way: by being a little bit of an asshole but smart enough to pull it off.

SAGITTARIUS

You'll use your humor to your advantage. Everyone knows Sagittarius is the funniest sign in the zodiac. One day this will play out in a major way. It might not mean getting your own show on Comedy Central, but your humor is what makes you so likable, and doors open for likable people. Whether it's a promotion, an amazing job, or the right partnership, the opportunity will be a result of your ability to make people laugh.

CAPRICORN

Your shrewdness will allow you to do what others can't (or won't). Most people get stuck behind their ideals and they can't see the forest for the trees. They want to be a lawyer because they saw *Ally McBeal*, or they want to be an FBI agent because it looked cool on *X-Files*. Capricorns have the gift of being hardcore realists and they don't think this way. They'll see a hole in the market and they'll attack.

AQUARIUS

You'll become the well-paid executive director of a nonprofit or start a business that centers around helping others. In short, your gigantic heart and love for helping others will reap financial returns. Of course, that's not why Aquarians set out to help people, but it's nice to know that karma works sometimes and that good things happen to good people.

PISCES

You'll create viral artwork. Whether it's a popular book, song, restaurant, or craft of another kind, Pisces are born artists. They're often content to make almost *no* money as long as they get to do work that seems meaningful and makes them happy. Even Pisces with professional jobs feel most themselves when work is over and they get to work on the side project about which they're truly passionate. This is why most successful artists are Pisces: Whether the money ever comes or not, they'd be doing the same thing.

Here's Why You're The Black Sheep Of Your Family

BASED ON YOUR ZODIAC SIGN

ARIES

They're tired of being long-distance. Aries are the least likely sign to stick around their hometown after graduation. They *need* something new and see every city as an adventure they have to take part in. This results in their family feeling left behind or like some bland precursor to when your life *actually* starts. Sure, it's their fault for having a (small) inferiority complex, but you can help them out by reassuring them with semi-frequent trips home.

TAURUS

They're tired of you not showing up to family events. Taureans are so independent that they don't hover around the nest when they leave; once they learn to walk, they run. They're totally self-sufficient and they only attend family gatherings because they truly look forward to seeing people—not out of guilt or obligation or to ask for money as they walk out the door. This can get interpreted by people as being aloof or not having a strong family connection, even though it's far from the truth.

GEMINI

They're tired of investing in projects you abandon months (and sometimes weeks) later. Geminis are *those* people who always have an exciting investment opportunity for their friends and family. They aren't grifters (just the opposite; Geminis are generally pure of heart), but it's just that there are SO many exciting things Geminis want to do, and when they're in the moment they all *seem* like they're going to pan out. But inevitably they are cast aside for the *next* exciting thing Geminis become obsessed with.

CANCER

They are tired of dealing with your sappy attitude. Cancers will cry during *The Notebook*, but they will also cry during the NBA Finals. There is no occasion where Cancers will not make it about their ~emotions~. They can also be insecure, overly sensitive, and a stick in the mud with other family members who like poking fun at people or telling mildly controversial jokes.

LEO

They're tired of your constant need for attention. Though it's usually subtle, one trait every Leo shares is that they need to be praised for their actions. This is one of the reasons your family exists, and they don't mind doing it once in a while, but it can get exhausting. You can help them out by having them communicate praise to you in writing or writing what they say down after you get off the phone. When you're feeling low, consult your written evidence instead of digging for more.

VIRGO

They're tired of you being better than them. Most people struggle to figure their lives out, but Virgos generally have an easier time at least covering the basics because they are very practical, intelligent, and focused. They're good at their jobs and they know how to make a budget—if you're the younger cousin or sibling of a Virgo, there's a reason you feel inferior.

LIBRA

They're tired of you not siding with them. Libras tend to be hated by immature family members and old high-school friends who assume loyalty should always fall with them in any dis-agreement—even when they're in the wrong. What they don't understand is that Libras are fair to a fault. Libras will admit when they are wrong in a fight, and they'll side with the person they genuinely feel is on the right side, "loyalty" be damned.

SCORPIO

They're tired of you bringing up politics at the dinner table. As a Scorpio, you're not afraid of conflict; in fact, it's your favorite pastime. When you bring up politics at the table, you're *hoping* for some exciting intellectual sparring—the kind not everyone else is comfortable with. To them, it's a danger zone of exactly the arguments they've been trying to avoid with the less *ahem* intellectual family members who join the conversation.

SAGITTARIUS

They're tired of you not taking anything seriously. Sure, Sagittarians are funny as fuck, but there's more to life than humor. Sometimes people want to have a serious conversation with you (or at least among themselves without you butting in). Occasionally, try holding the comic relief until after the moment of sincerity has passed.

CAPRICORN

They're tired of being nagged. Capricorns can be powerhouses in getting shit done, but they have the horrible habit of *both* preferring not to do things alone *and* always knowing their way is best. This means their partner in crime usually becomes their servant in crime. And yes, the outcome is perfect—but that's not the point. Lighten up a little.

AQUARIUS

They're tired of you hitting them up for money for different causes. Aquarians have giant hearts, and there is no shortage of good causes they get involved with over the course of their lives. Unfortunately, other people don't see these charities as the big priority that an Aquarians do, and after a while saying "no" to being asked to volunteer or lend financial support gets awkward.

PISCES

They just don't "get" you. Pisces tend to be total outcasts from their families because they are sensitive, artistic souls who prefer to be alone and don't *need* the approval of those around them. Growing up, they spent a lot of time alone in their room listening to "alarming" music of one variety or another. It's not that you don't love your family; it's that you're all very different people and it hasn't been important enough to you yet to bridge the gap, at least not yet.

Here's Exactly What Would Happen To You In A Horror Movie

BASED ON YOUR ZODIAC SIGN

ARIES

The whole rule of "never explore strange noises in the basement/woods/haunted attic" was created for Aries people of the world. They are brave and adventurous to a fault. When a serial killer is on the loose, they won't play it safe and will eventually be axed when they go off on their own to investigate.

TAURUS

Tauruses will nearly make it to the end, but their demise will be due to their independence. At some point someone will tell Taurus what they should do for their own safety, and Taurus will think, "Who the fuck are you?" and do the opposite. In scary movies, there's safety in numbers.

GEMINI

Geminis will DEFINITELY be one of the first people to die. They see the good in everyone, so they'll be the one basically trying to make friends with the killer as he's killing them. RIP, Gemini.

CANCER

Sweet, sweet Cancer might survive if they surround themselves with one or two stronger friends, but if they're on their own—lol, no. Cancers are lovers, not fighters, and they'll be murdered doing something cool like going for a midnight swim (water sign, yo) or making love to their honey.

LEO

TBH, Leos would probably end up being the killer. They are smart and creative enough to pull it off, and they'd love the attention that came with their infamous death.

VIRGO

Virgos would not survive a horror movie. It's hard to imagine Virgos being so impractical as to find themselves in any setting where a horror movie would take place. They would never get lost on an abandoned road or feel tempted to explore an abandoned insane asylum, and they're savvy enough with real-estate transactions not to purchase a house that was built on cursed burial ground. They are the minor character we are only introduced to in order to see them get spectacularly murdered.

LIBRA

Libras would probably survive a horror movie. They are too well-liked to be anyone's target, and they are smart enough to figure out how to get out of a bad situation.

SCORPIO

Scorpios would survive a horror movie, but only because they are willing to put up a hard fight to get through it. Scorpios are not frail. They will fight tooth and nail to survive.

SAGITTARIUS

Let's be honest: We all love Sagittarian people, but they definitely aren't going to survive. They'll be the comic relief dude/chick that cracks jokes through the whole movie and then dies in a scary-but-hilarious way like drinking a beer bong full of blood.

CAPRICORN

Capricorns would not survive a horror movie. They are shrewd and adept, sure, but they also have a likability problem. They are the accountant that gets murdered after yelling at a sweet old lady for being too slow. Everyone in the audience cheers when they die.

AQUARIUS

Aquarians' sense of humanity is their downfall. They are the person who picks up hitchhikers or stops to help someone who falls down and then gets murdered. The every-man-or-woman-for-themselves mantra you need to survive a horror movie would not appeal to Aquarius.

PISCES

Pisces would survive a horror movie. They would be the quiet genius you don't pay attention to until the end. Pisces are creative and underrated, so they'd notice ways to get out or hide that other people wouldn't see—they can also kill a bitch if need be.

The Type Of Person Who's Attracted To You

BASED ON YOUR ZODIAC SIGN

ARIES
The people who are attracted to Aries are the ones that crave adventure. They see Aries as brave thrill-seekers who can pull them out of their shell and make them brave, too. People attracted to Aries will be doers; couch potatoes will pick a different sign. They want an Aries partner because they are vivacious people who don't want to lead a quiet life and "grow old." They know that with an Aries, life will always continue to be new and fun.

Qualities: fun-loving, happy to be second in command, laid-back/go-with-the-flow type.

TAURUS
The people who are attracted to Taurus crave loyalty. They know that when Tauruses make up their minds to love someone, it's not going to change. They also know that Tauruses prefer to be laid-back instead of dramatic and that they tend to be intelligent people. Their suitors are similarly laid-back people who will appreciate how dependable they are.

Qualities: emotionally mature, financially secure, patient.

GEMINI

The people who are attracted to Geminis crave excitement. They love that Geminis are always, always, *always* excited about something—even if that something changes from week to week (and sometimes hour to hour). They want a Gemini partner because they want their life to constantly include new things: passions, projects, and dreams.

Qualities: happy, open-minded, and more casual than formal.

CANCER

People who are attracted to Cancers crave love. They know that Cancers are a solid foundation on which they can build their future. These are people who are in it for the long haul. Also, Cancerians tend to attract rich partners because their ambivalence about wealth assures their love interest that they aren't in it for the money.

Qualities: sensual, deep, an "old soul."

LEO

The people who are attracted to Leos crave a star. They want to be around someone so creative and smart and *cool*. Dating Leos is like dating the head cheerleader or the quarterback of the football team; there's a bit of intrigue about someone so bright and shiny who would actually date a mortal.

Qualities: giving, good communicators, generous, submissive.

VIRGO

The people who are attracted to Virgos crave a safe place to land. They love that Virgos are always put-together and suffer less from the adult kid syndrome of their peers. Especially to people in their 20s, Virgos are very attractive because of their ability to figure out things that seem complicated to others.

Unfortunately, Virgos can get stuck in a bad habit of dating fixer-uppers who want to use them for this ability.

Qualities: fly by the seat of their pants, fun-loving, charismatic.

LIBRA
The people who are attracted to Libras crave an equal partner in life. Libras are adept at almost everything they do, especially anything that requires emotional intelligence. They draw in people who want the best for themselves—a high-quality partner who will upgrade their life in all ways.

Qualities: ambitious, introverted, warm-hearted.

SCORPIO
The people who are attracted to Scorpios crave raw passion. No one comes close to the intensity and focus Scorpios have when they have a goal in mind. Who can blame someone for wondering what it would be like if that passion were directed towards them? People know that life will never be boring or commonplace when they are with Scorpio.

Qualities: genuine, intelligent, sensual.

SAGITTARIUS
The people who are attracted to Sagittarians crave someone who can make them laugh. They know that Sagittarius is not only the funniest sign in the zodiac but that they are incredible friends and partners as well. Their suitors are people who are looking for a best friend as well as a romantic partner.

Qualities: laid-back, conservative, humorous.

CAPRICORN
The people who are attracted to Capricorns are pragmatists who crave a refined partner. They know that Capricorns can give them something few other signs could: someone with great

taste who is dependable and unlikely to ever embarrass themselves or spill a secret. Capricorns attract traditional people who want the best things in life.

Qualities: more formal than casual, ambitious, intelligent, not overly sensitive or sensual.

AQUARIUS

The people who are attracted to Aquarius people crave a life filled with meaning. They know that the driving force behind Aquarians is their need to do good and help the people around them. They can't help but be attracted to and inspired by their generous spirit.

Qualities: generous, sensitive, a deep feeler.

PISCES

The people who are attracted to Pisces crave creativity. They know that Pisces are deep, old souls who live artistic lives filled with good food, art, and music. They are attracted to the idea of a lifelong partnership with someone who can help them express themselves through all forms of art.

Qualities: intelligent, introverted, sensual.

The Telltale Sign You *Really* Like Someone

BASED ON YOUR ZODIAC SIGN

 ### ARIES
You slow down to make sure someone else is comfortable and happy.

Aries are adventurous and independent. They're used to doing their own thing and are generally unafraid of what might go wrong. They're not used to people tagging along (because they might slow the adventure down) and even less used to actually caring that the person is there. When an Aries *really* likes you, they're willing to go at a slower pace because they want you to feel as safe as they do and share the experience with them.

 ### TAURUS
You'll let them in.

Taurus people can live in gated communities of their own design—they will only let you enter when you've proven yourself completely. Once they know you aren't there to steal their independence or wrong them, they will be able to let their stubborn selves be vulnerable and share pieces of their inner self with you.

GEMINI

You'll stick with them when they go through a hard time.

Geminis are passionate and fun-loving; they want love to be an exciting adventure. The way you can tell they really care about you is that they don't leave when the party's over. You've earned a special place in their heart when they nurture you when you're sick and want to hear about your bad day.

CANCER

You let them do something nice for *you*.

Cancers are obsessed with nurturing others. They are always concerned about making people feel good to the extent where someone might even have a difficult time finding an opening to return the favor. Only when Cancers are really into someone will they feel comfortable enough to stop filling every interaction with charitable acts and allow themselves to feel nurtured as well.

LEO

You give them *all* the attention.

When in love, we often do something called "mirroring"; we give people affection the way we wish we received it. For Leos, there is one currency to rule them all: attention. When they love someone, they heap attention on them. They laugh at their jokes, compliment them, and make them the star of the show—if only because this is their preferred method of being courted.

VIRGO

You suddenly become okay with a little messy spontaneity.

It goes against all Virgo urges to leave things unplanned, un-done, or unknown—but they will do it for people they *really* like. Virgos with a serious crush become Virgos with the su-perhuman power of knowing things should be planned better but suddenly not caring. This isn't because they are trying to appear chill to win someone over; it's because they genuinely care more about someone else's happiness than about their own overachiever tendencies.

LIBRA
You fight with them.

Libras love harmony in all their relationships. While they are super-fair, they still have trouble with conflict because they don't like upsetting people. You know Libra really wants you around when they go through the trouble of fighting with you. It means they want things to get better between the two of you, and it's worth the drama of conflict to have you around.

SCORPIO
You're selfless.

Traditionally associated with selfishness, Scorpios prefer to think of their ruthlessness as a practical attribute: They get shit done. Only for someone they are *truly* interested in will they cast aside this practicality and wade into the messiness that is a relationship.

SAGITTARIUS
You try to make them laugh.

For Sagittarians, there is no better way to show someone you love them than by showing off one of their best assets: They're funny as fuck. They'll stop at nothing to make the object of their affection start belly-laughing.

CAPRICORN
You have more fun than you can remember having.

Capricorns take so much pride in becoming successful and having a put-together life and home that they can forget to take advantage of the moment and YOLO once in a while. Having a crush brings out their fun-loving side, and they suddenly become someone who is always smiling. It's pretty cute.

AQUARIUS
You try to get them involved in a cause you care about.

Aquarians are the humanitarians of the zodiac and are always volunteering or learning about politics or doing something that benefits other people. They express love through their deep understanding and concern for the world as a whole. When they really like someone, they want them to be a part of their mission in life. They want a partner in making a legacy.

PISCES
You create art for them.

Pisces are deeply creative people, no matter what form their art takes: music, writing, cooking, or crafting. When they like someone they will do something Pisces only do rarely and attempt to unveil their sacred inner world to this new person through sharing their art. Maybe they will make them a playlist on Spotify they slaved over for hours, share a poem they've written, or learn one of their favorite songs on guitar. Whatever it is, the recipient should be aware this isn't something the attention-shy Pisces is eager to do; it's a moment to be respected and treasured.

The Best Compliment Someone Could Give You

BASED ON YOUR ZODIAC SIGN

ARIES

"There is no way you won't be incredibly successful in life."

TAURUS

"You're the most thoughtful person I've ever met."

GEMINI

"You are a deeply creative genius."

CANCER

*"You love me better
than anyone else is capable of."*

LEO

"I admire you."

VIRGO

*"You're so smart, it's hard
to keep up with your intellect."*

LIBRA

*"I don't know how I'd figure out any of
my problems if it weren't for you."*

SCORPIO

"I could never have too much of you."[1]

---

1 In the case of Scorpio, this is a bit redundant, because every compliment you give
them is the best compliment you could give them.

SAGITTARIUS

*"There is never a boring day
when you're around."*

CAPRICORN

*"You are the most intelligent and adept
partner I could ask for."*

AQUARIUS

*"There is more good in the world
because you were born."*

PISCES

*"You're much deeper
than most people."*

ARIES

♈

DATES	March 21 – April 19
SIGN	Ram
RULING PLANET	Mars
ZODIAC QUALITY	Cardinal
ELEMENT	Fire
POSITIVE TRAITS	Energetic, Independent, Adventurous
NEGATIVE TRAITS	Self-Centered, Shallow, Rude

IF ARIES WAS...

A STARBUCKS DRINK:
Eggnog Latte

A COLOR:
Bright Red

A GREEK GOD:
Zeus—king and father of the gods. The ruler of lightning, thunder.

AN ADDICTION:
Caffeine

AN ALCOHOLIC BEVERAGE:
Vodka & Red Bull

A DRUG:
Steroids

IN A HIGH-SCHOOL CLIQUE:
Jocks

A CITY:
Chicago, Illinois

A HARRY POTTER HOUSE:
Slytherin

AN UNTRANSLATABLE FRENCH WORD:
Cartonner—something that has had huge success

A KISS:
Rough

A TEEN MOVIE:
Mean Girls

A CLOTHING ITEM:
Leather Jacket

A FAMOUS LANDMARK:
Mount Everest

A SEASON:
Summer

ARIES

PERSONALITY TRAITS

ARIES ARE VERY PRIMAL IN NATURE due to being born as the first sign in the zodiac. They tend to resist analysis or attempts to explain them, and they represent the ego and free will in their purest form.

Aries are energetic and commanding, fiery and prophetic. They are referred to as the dynamo because they are so progressive and compelling. They will always simply choose to exist how they are rather than try to understand why they feel what they do and act how they do through the eyes of others. This self-assured nature causes Aries to become upset and overwhelmed when people do not see them the way they see themselves.

Like young children, Aries often tend to be spontaneous, frank, and open, but also self-centered and willful. Also like a child, they approach the world with an optimistic innocence.

Known to be natural adventurers, Aries will always feel a strong impulse to explore. They are also very fond of being the star wherever they go, and they shine very brightly in social situations. Their egos never need the approval of others, as they are so self-assured, but they do demand that those around them pay attention to them, because they know how much they have to offer others. Aries that do not slow down and reflect on their actions and feelings run the risk of breaking down emotionally when their self-confidence is undermined by those who do not listen.

Always known to be physical, the competitive Aries will need to explore their limits to feel like they are growing. They always need to be active and prefer it over introspection. They will not ruminate over a problem or a situation; they will swiftly try to problem-solve and quickly deal with everything the best way they see fit. When their attempts produce bad results, or if they are delayed in any way from jumping into action, Aries will suffer. This is often why they choose to withdraw from life periodically, giving them the ability to study and figure out a problem from a distance, with no risk of being talked out of action or convinced that they are wrong.

Aries have a very, very strong desire to lead. However, some people born on this month manifest that desire and do not take the right steps to nurture it. Some will feel so strongly about being first, and they will not focus on being a leader, which causes them to come off as selfish and unfit. This causes them to feel frustrated and even guilty. They will often hold within them a very intense form of self-pity. However, when Aries take their leadership skills and put aside the need to bolster through life, they are truly the most idealistic, original, and successful sign of the zodiac.

ARIES

COMPATIBILITY & RELATIONSHIPS

ARIES ARE ADVENTUROUS RISK-TAKERS who prefer new and novel experiences. They are great partners for other adventurous signs (Sagittarius, Leo) and those who prefer to let someone else take the wheel and are happy to be along for the ride (Libra). The keyword in this relationship is "adventure partner." People who are looking to stay home most nights (looking at you, Taurus and Cancer) will get exhausted by Aries's need for excitement.

ARIES AND ARIES COMPATIBILITY: Aries and Aries will have a solid foundation of fun and friendship. They will challenge each other and know how to keep the other one interested, but they'll lack the balance and depth of being paired with someone who complements them rather than replicates them.

ARIES AND TAURUS COMPATIBILITY: Aries will be annoyed that homebody Taurus likes to relax more than adventure out into the world, and Taurus will be annoyed that they aren't in control of the relationship. These two have different values and different personalities, so it's hard for them to get close and feel like they have a real connection.

ARIES AND GEMINI COMPATIBILITY: Aries and Gemini make an exciting couple that is always out of the house doing something fun together. They are the opposite of the "Netflix + Chill" homebody couple. Their Instagram feed makes most people exhausted, but they love living an active, adventurous life together.

ARIES AND CANCER COMPATIBILITY: This is a difficult relationship, as Aries will always feel slowed down by their Cancer, and Cancer will always feel like they can't relax around Aries. They have different values and different dispositions—and not necessarily in a complementary way. However, with the right people this relationship can work—Aries will inject excitement into Cancer's life and draw them out of their shell, and Cancer will help Aries venture into their own minds and get in touch with their emotional needs.

ARIES AND LEO COMPATIBILITY: Aries and Leo are natural allies and make great friends. They love to try new things together, go on adventures, be silly, and challenge themselves. As a couple, they have a large circle of friends and are always telling wild stories about their travels together.

ARIES AND VIRGO COMPATIBILITY: This is a natural pairing of two complementary people. Aries will pick the adventure, and Virgo will plan it out. They will challenge and balance each other and genuinely make the other person's life better.

ARIES AND LIBRA COMPATIBILITY: This is a relationship of two alphas, which can make it pretty challenging, but when it works they are a force to be reckoned with. They will be a power couple with a lively (and large) group of friends they adore.

ARIES AND SCORPIO COMPATIBILITY: This is a toxic combination. They are both hotheads who are quick to anger and slow to apologize. They are also both competitive and strive to be the dominant ones in relationships.

ARIES AND SAGITTARIUS COMPATIBILITY: These signs make a fun-loving couple who are always making each other laugh. They have a ton of inside jokes and prefer to keep things in their lives light and happy. They have a big circle of friends and are always planning fun things for everyone to do.

ARIES AND CAPRICORN COMPATIBILITY: There's not a lot that Aries and Capricorn have in common, and both types aren't the kind of person to slow their roll for someone else. Capricorns are more conservative and want to protect what they put out into the world more than Aries's look-before-you-leap nature allows them. Aries's least favorite thing in the world is feeling like someone is holding them back, so they'll also struggle with Capricorn in trying to control them.

ARIES AND AQUARIUS COMPATIBILITY: These two will get lost in conversation with each other a lot. Long into their relationship, they have nights where they stay up talking until sunrise. They're on the same mental level, and they both have a lot of interests and things that excite them. They'll be able to form a solid foundation of friendship on which to build a relationship.

ARIES AND PISCES COMPATIBILITY: This combination isn't the strongest, as they struggle in communication. Pisces might drop hints about what they want and need, but they will never straight-up say it. Aries need that clarity. Both partners just can't figure out or fake being what the other person needs.

HOW TO ATTRACT ARIES

Aries need to chase the apple of its eye, so the best way to attract one would be to play hard to get. Not only will this pique their interest, it will cater to their need for competition. Getting you as a prize will be rewarding, but be sure to give them the chance to catch you. If not, Aries will get discouraged and move on to a fresh, new conquest.

HOW TO KNOW IF ARIES LIKES YOU

Aries will try to touch you a lot if they like you, so expect a lot of hugs. As a naturally competitive person, you will be challenged by Aries. If they like you, they will want you to prove yourself by playing one of their games, so accept the challenge and stand your ground. If Aries get upset or jealous when they see you flirting with someone else, you can be sure that they are interested in you. Aries will often think about you and will therefore ask you questions about your day; they will want to know what is going on in your general life. This is their way of keeping up with you and showing an interest in you. However, the great thing about Aries is that they will often just tell you that they are fond of you—they tend to be quite straightforward.

WHAT ARIES ARE LIKE IN A RELATIONSHIP

Aries are insanely flirtatious, and they will always take initiative when it comes to romancing the person who's captured their interest. They are filled with passion and a need for adventure, and they bring a lot of excitement and energy to a relationship. Once in love, Aries will be committed for life. The best, most long-lasting relationships for Aries always incorporate spice and activities that keep their fire burning. Every day with Aries will be different and filled with thrills, and they will make sure that their love will never be boring or average.

ARIES'S IDEAL DATE

Aries are the epitome of spontaneity, so a surprise trip would be the absolute best date in their books. They admire people who help them to experience new things, so changing up their routine and doing something out of the ordinary is always exciting for Aries. Choose a place they have never been and don't plan anything. Explore together, learn together, and simply have fun living in the moment. They will absolutely love it.

ARIES IN THE BEDROOM

Aries will keep you guessing. Always. You will never know what they are going to do next, and they tend to be quite bold, rough, and dominant. Due to their competitive nature, they will like to challenge themselves in bed and won't stop until they please you.

HOW ARIES DEAL WITH HEARTBREAK

Aries will never admit that they care when a relationship ends. However, they truly do. Underneath their strong, brash nature is an underlying lack of confidence and a fear that they may be unworthy of love. They will work to convince everyone around them that they are doing just fine, and they will often commit to a lot of new things to forget about how hurt they are.

HOW ARIES ARE AS FRIENDS

Having Aries as a best friend means that you are going to have a lot of fun, as they are the epitome of playful and adventurous. The most normal, boring day will turn into something spectacular with them. Since they are highly observant, nothing will ever get past Aries, so do not deceive or lie to them. Befriending Aries means that you are in store for a lot of sarcastic, witty humor, and though they may joke around a lot, Aries will always respect and appreciate you. They are some of the most loyal friends in the zodiac.

HOW TO GAIN THE RESPECT OF ARIES

Aries love a straight shooter and an independent person. If you have a life outside of your friendship or relationship with Aries, they will respect you deeply.

HOW ARIES ARE WHEN THEY'RE MAD

Aries are babies, to put it bluntly. They will explode and never think about how their words and actions affect the people around them. They will never sugarcoat their feelings and will often verbally hurt people they care about to protect their pride. If Aries is angry with you, simply staying quiet and not reacting to their reactive state is the best possible way to cool them down. They will calm down quickly, and they will often feel extremely guilty for getting out of hand.

HOW ARIES ARE WHEN THEY'RE SAD

You know Aries are sad when they don't get worked up about things that would normally make them angry. As very reactive people, when sad Aries will skip the rage and often turn to impulsivity. They will be noticeably toned down, with less vigor than usual.

SIMPLE THINGS THAT MAKE ARIES HAPPY

Aries love being listened to, especially when they don't ask for it. They like when people take notice of what they need. When they don't feel very good about themselves, being around a good friend or doing something athletic will always make Aries happy.

ARIES AT THEIR BEST

Aries are knowledge-seeking and born leaders. They are so much more than they appear to be and will always be able to take on many roles and forms in their relationships. They will always be the happy, optimistic ones when things get tough, and they will inspire people in that sense to see the bright side of things.

ARIES AT THEIR WORST

Aries tend to be rude. They revert to using bad language and insults when provoked in any situation and will always play the Devil's advocate. They tend to use their strengths in the wrong ways, which is why they are often so internally conflicted.

WHAT ARIES FEAR THE MOST

Aries are conflicted all the time. They want adventure, but they also want peace. They don't want a boring life, but they want to make sure that their relationships and companionships are long-lasting and not just fleeting. Their insecurity causes them to live in perpetual fear of being broken up with or left by a best friend.

LIKELY OCCUPATIONS FOR ARIES

Aries are extremely competitive and strong-willed. Their vibrant nature and enthusiasm allow for them to excel in commission-based jobs. Their impulsive tendencies often cause them to be fearless and brave, setting them up to be police officers, firefighters, and other everyday heroes. Aries also make amazing entrepreneurs, soldiers, or politicians.

LIKELY HEALTH CONCERNS FOR ARIES

Aries are ruled by their head. Therefore, they are prone to headaches and very painful migraines. Aries on the go are often stressed, prone to accidents, and their bodies are usually beaten up and in need of rest.

WHERE TO TAKE ARIES ON VACATION

Aries will always enjoy going somewhere they have never been. However, they are so competitive, they often want to vacation somewhere under the radar. If you want to take Aries on vacation, take them to an obscure island—somewhere you can barely find on a map. Make sure this place boasts a lot of things to physically challenge Aries such as mountains, cliffs, etc.

ARIES'S LEARNING STYLE

Aries learn through their experiences. They jump right into uncharted territory, and this impulsivity teaches them everything they need to know. As a sign that thirsts for knowledge, Aries will never back down from learning something new.

ARIES'S KIND OF HUMOR

Aries have a very goofy and physical approach to humor. They are extremely witty and are some of the funniest people in the zodiac.

ARIES'S FAVORITE PASTIME

Anything athletic or competitive. Aries are also fond of singing and joking around—karaoke is a guilty pleasure!

WHAT TO SAY TO MOTIVATE YOUR ARIES

Don't ever forget just how strong you are—in your mind, in your emotions, and physically. You have the ability to move mountains with your heart and your words because you operate on such a level of extreme passion. Don't ever lose touch of that. You are capable of so much, and you will always come out on top if you just remind yourself of that every single day.

TAURUS

DATES	April 20 – May 21
SIGN	Bull
RULING PLANET	Earth
ZODIAC QUALITY	Fixed
ELEMENT	Earth
POSITIVE TRAITS	Loyal, Stable, Sensual
NEGATIVE TRAITS	Stubborn, Selfish, Emotionally Closed-Off

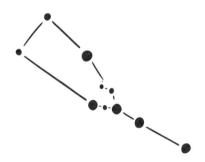

IF TAURUS WAS...

A STARBUCKS DRINK:
Cinnamon Dolce Latte

A COLOR:
Earthy Brown

A GREEK GOD:
Dionysus—the god of wine, parties, festivals, and indulgence

AN ADDICTION:
Binge-Eating

AN ALCOHOLIC BEVERAGE:
Red Wine

A DRUG:
Ecstasy

IN A HIGH-SCHOOL CLIQUE:
Artsy Kids

A CITY:
Paris, France

A HARRY POTTER HOUSE:
Hufflepuff

AN UNTRANSLATABLE FRENCH WORD:
Péripatéticien—the constant wanderer

A KISS:
Romantic

A TEEN MOVIE:
Sixteen Candles

A CLOTHING ITEM:
Sweatpants

A FAMOUS LANDMARK:
Big Ben

A SEASON:
Fall

TAURUS

PERSONALITY TRAITS

TAURUSES ARE THE BEST REPRESENTATION OF GROWTH and development in the zodiac. This is why Taureans are often considered to be very rooted and earthy nurturers. They are highly caring and compassionate.

Every Taurus needs harmony in their life. They are constantly concerned with making everything around them pleasurable and lovely to look at. They are deeply material, and their happiness relies on possessions and security in their lifestyle. Taurus's need for harmony often causes them to be quite flexible, though they are known for being extremely stubborn. They often struggle to find a balance, but their internal quest for simplicity helps them find symmetry in their personality.

As very airy and changeable individuals, Tauruses often struggle to find their autonomy. It is very important for them to develop independence and to learn how to take care of themselves without the help of others. In order to do so, Tauruses must understand that the world does not revolve around them and that they cannot always be the center of attention. They have to learn how to develop healthy habits alone.

Tauruses will never say no to indulging in the most physical matters. They love food deeply, are very sexual creatures, and enjoy sports. However, they do not crave constant activity, often needing to recharge and relax after a long day. Tauruses will generally prefer to stay home, where things are comfortable and familiar and simple.

Tauruses boasts strong observational skills. They have the ability to map out, strategize, and solve problems or implement plans. However, they are known to procrastinate, because they do not always need to be in action. Finding a balance between relaxing and working extremely hard is often a struggle for Tauruses, as they love both sides equally but do not crave them at the same time. It is either action or inaction, work or comfort.

A natural-born team leader, Tauruses enjoys team work when they are in charge and have the ability to add individual touches to the project. They are dominant and will fight back urges to lead when they are not in a position that allows them to do so. Their stubborn nature is combative here, and they will often argue until things are done their way.

Taureans can be considered quite selfish due to their stubbornness and their strong beliefs. They always protect their own interests above anything else to ensure their comfort. However, they are highly intuitive and can be people-pleasers because of that. They take it to heart when they see people who need a compassionate hand and will always live for the people they care about.

TAURUS

COMPATIBILITY & RELATIONSHIPS

TAURUSES ARE VERY INDULGENT, creative, and lazy. They are best suited for someone who doesn't mind relaxing and staying in a few nights a week, while still catering to their creativity and physicality. Cancer are amazing matches for Tauruses, because they will relate to a Taurean's need for security and deep, serious relationships. Cancer are also empaths who are compassionate, so they will appreciate and love Taureans' sensitivity and need for emotionality.

TAURUS AND ARIES COMPATIBILITY: Aries will be annoyed that homebody Tauruses like to relax more than adventure out into the world, and Tauruses will be annoyed that they aren't in control of the relationship. These two have different values and personalities, so it's hard for them to get too close and feel like they have a real connection.

TAURUS AND TAURUS COMPATIBILITY: More than most other signs, Taurus's values are very important to them. Having someone with the same values (loyalty, consistency, comfort) already starts this relationship off on a good foot. These two people know how to take care of each other, and they have a super-solid foundation knowing how trustworthy the person they love is.

TAURUS AND GEMINI COMPATIBILITY: Tauruses prize loyalty and stability above all else, which feels stifling to any Gemini they date. Similarly, Tauruses find Gemini's ways chaotic and unpredictable. These signs stress each other out!

TAURUS AND CANCER COMPATIBILITY: This has the potential to be one of the best matches in the zodiac. Taurus and Cancer are similar people with complementary values. They will enjoy building a happy home life together, having an extremely loyal and supportive partner, and spoiling each other with physical touch, comforting meals, and endless affection.

TAURUS AND LEO COMPATIBILITY: Jealousy will be a big problem in this relationship, as Taurus will never be comfortable with Leo's need for attention. Taurus will never feel like they are able to relax, and Leo will feel like they are constantly walking on eggshells.

TAURUS AND VIRGO COMPATIBILITY: What most people describe as "boring," this couple will describe as "ideal." They are on the same page about many things in life, from finances to where they want to be in five years. They will support each other and make each other feel fully confident in the relationship.

TAURUS AND LIBRA COMPATIBILITY: There's a lot of potential for jealousy in this relationship, but it can work if Libra babies Taurus a bit and always makes it known that they are their number-one priority. Initially Taurus will think Libra is too flashy, but as soon as they are exposed to their softer side they will be won over. Similarly, Libra will love the sturdy foundation Taurus provides.

TAURUS AND SCORPIO COMPATIBILITY: This is arguably the worst combination of any two signs. This pair just seems to bring out the absolute worst in each other, like a tornado coming into each other's lives and just ruining everything about the other person. There are some people who just shouldn't be together, and this duo is toxic.

TAURUS AND SAGITTARIUS COMPATIBILITY: These signs make great friends, as they can appreciate fun and indulgence together, but they don't often make great couples. People born under Taurus tend to want to settle down, while Sagittarians tend to want to drift around. They aren't naturally suited to complement each other.

TAURUS AND CAPRICORN COMPATIBILITY: Taurus and Capricorn are natural allies. They both love to indulge in the finer things in life, are ambitious, and like to show off a little bit. They fit together well and can be a very happy "power couple."

TAURUS AND AQUARIUS COMPATIBILITY: This is an unlikely pairing of people who see the world very differently. Aquarians' wacky ideas can feel exhausting for Taurus, while Taurus can feel too boring for Aquarius.

TAURUS AND PISCES COMPATIBILITY: This is a wonderful match, pairing a dreamer (Pisces) with a realist (Taurus). They both prefer a laid-back lifestyle and know the other person needs to be supported and loved. They will have one of the happiest home lives and be a couple with an unshakeable bond.

HOW TO ATTRACT TAURUS

To attract Taurus, you simply have to do something thoughtful for them. Pay attention to their emotional and physical needs to show them that you are also an empath. When Taurus sees how kind and compassionate you are, they melt and open up to reciprocate that kindness. When you prove to them just how thoughtful you are, they trust you more and see you as a suitable mate that will complement their nurturing side.

HOW TO KNOW IF TAURUS LIKES YOU

When Taurus likes you, they will ask you for your thoughts on a lot of things, and they will engage you in stimulating conversation. They are nurturers, so if you see them getting protective over you, it is a good sign that they are fond of you and want to keep you safe. They appreciate your quirks and will notice things that others don't about you. When Taurus makes fun of you, know that it is good-natured and is their playful way of showing interest. Taurus will always complement the apple of their eye and can be extremely sweet when they admire someone. It is unfortunate, because they often fear that their sensitivity will lead them to be rejected or hurt. If you notice Taurus doing any of the above, nurture them back. Make them understand that you, too, are interested, because they can discourage themselves and end up guarding their advances.

WHAT TAURUSES ARE LIKE IN A RELATIONSHIP

In a relationship, Taureans are very traditional in the sense that they will love going out on dates. However, they are also homebodies, so a lot of your time will be spent cuddling up to them in bed and watching movie marathons with them on the couch. Taurus will fight to maintain a good relationship and put in a lot of effort when it comes to someone they love. Taurus will make you feel secure and cared for in a relationship and will always fight to protect your heart and your feelings. However, they can be stubborn, so it is very important to nurture good communication early on to ensure that the easily hurt bull doesn't get offended or guarded when you bring up something that disappointed you or made you angry.

TAURUS'S IDEAL DATE

Taurus loves the finer things in life and also adores going out to eat or try new beverages. Therefore, taking them on a wine or beer tasting would be an absolutely wonderful date. Tasting wine, eating delicious food, and enjoying the environment around them will appeal to every sensual side of Taurus while complementing their need for physical stimulation.

HOW TAURUSES ARE IN THE BEDROOM

Tauruses are quite harmonized in bed. They tend to be very sensual and deep, but they can also be very direct and dominant. If they had to choose, they would always pick "making love" rather than just having sex or getting the deed done. They want to feel loved in bed and refuse to hook up casually. They adore neck kisses, deep embraces, closeness, and romance in the bedroom and are known to be very sexually charged, magnetic lovers.

HOW TAURUSES DEAL WITH HEARTBREAK

Tauruses hate change. They absolutely despise it. If they have been in a relationship for a long time, it will also take a long time for them to get accustomed to being single again. They will often suffer from extreme insecurity and pain when they have their heart broken, feeling unworthy of love during the healing process. However, Taureans have a way of putting up a very deceiving front and will often keep all of their sad and dark feelings inside of them to maintain their nonchalance. Taureans often suffer from heartbreak behind closed doors, and they can feel so intensely that they shut down completely when rejected or mourning the loss of love.

HOW TAURUSES ARE AS FRIENDS

When you have Taurus as a best friend, they are the perfect travel buddy. They will never say no to a road trip or a fun little beach vacation. Tauruses will bring to your friendship their calm nature and will give the best advice. Their ambition and their creativity will inspire you and ignite your passions. The great thing about a Taurean best friend is that they will appreciate you and accept you for your faults rather than judging you for them.

HOW TO GAIN THE RESPECT OF TAURUS

The most impressive thing for Tauruses is someone who is simply honest and real. They hate fake people. They love reliable presences in their life and will respect those who are not flaky. Gain huge points with Tauruses by letting them do their thing at their own pace—they hate to be rushed and really appreciate people who let them take their time.

HOW TAURUSES ARE WHEN THEY'RE MAD

Tauruses will never blow up on you right away. When mad, they will often give you subtle, passive-aggressive hints. They will become silent and cold, keeping everything in until it boils over and causes them to explode with emotions. Physical creatures, they often use their body, pacing and waving their hands, exhausting themselves in an angry fit. However, it is very hard to upset Tauruses, as they tend to be rational and don't want to disturb any harmony.

HOW TAURUSES ARE WHEN THEY'RE SAD

When sad, Tauruses will isolate themselves. They will turn to binge-eating and sleeping, and they will always play the victim in any situation. This allows them to further turn into their comforts and justify their descent into negative indulgence.

SIMPLE THINGS THAT MAKE TAURUSES HAPPY

Tauruses are happiest when they are eating good food. A simple night in with someone they love, eating treats and watching movies, is something they cherish.

TAURUSES AT THEIR BEST

Tauruses hold extraordinary potential, and they are extremely strong individuals. They take life as it comes and always find a way to roll with the punches. They are kind, very friendly, intelligent, funny creatures who hold a rare and beautiful sensitivity. They are revered by many different groups of people and are impressively creative.

TAURUSES AT THEIR WORST

Tauruses tend to deny responsibility when it comes to tough situations or problems. They never want to deal with anything and will ignore their faults. Tauruses also don't have a very strong backbone when it comes to sticking up for themselves, so they will try to get out of issues to avoid conflict. This causes a lot of anxiety for them and creates more problems in the long run because they are always taking the easy way out.

WHAT TAURUSES FEAR THE MOST

Tauruses are very grounded and reliable. They crave harmony in their life. Therefore, they are terrified of being outside of their comfort zone, and they fear inconsistency the way some people fear physical things such as snakes or spiders. The idea of being challenged comfort-wise causes acute problems for a bull, like chest pain and emotional meltdowns.

TAURUS'S LIKELY OCCUPATIONS

Tauruses are very steadfast and stable human beings. They work extremely hard when it comes to guaranteed payoffs such as vacations, benefits, and great job security and salaries. They are determined, honest, and patient when they need to be, and they have a great approach to solving problems. Dependable and great leaders, Taureans would make amazing educators, lawyers, and designers. Because they are creative and love material things, they are often known to be very successful working with food, jewelry, and other luxury items.

TAURUS'S LIKELY HEALTH CONCERNS

Ruled by the throat, Taureans often suffer from throat infections, goiters, and problems with their thyroid.

WHERE TO TAKE TAURUSES ON VACATION

An ideal vacation for Tauruses involves comfort. They need to be pampered, taken care of, and they also need to experience delicious food and beautiful surroundings. Taking your Taurus to wine country and booking a swanky hotel room complete with spa and room service would be an amazing vacation idea, because it complements every aspect of the Taurean personality.

TAURUS'S LEARNING STYLE

Tauruses are very sensual learners. Therefore, they need a multitude of educational aids, like music, video, taste, touch, and smell. They are very hands-on and learn by being exposed to the actual material they are learning about rather than just reading about it in a textbook.

TAURUS'S HUMOR

Tauruses are very observational. They don't even realize they are being hilarious, because they take from their environment and simply build off its momentum. They never have a problem with laughing at themselves and are often the first to make a witty joke about something they did or a blunder they experienced.

TAURUS'S FAVORITE PASTIME

Tauruses loves to go on adventures, write, and act. However, they also love to do makeup and can often be found perusing the internet for tutorials and fun things to try.

WHAT TO SAY TO MOTIVATE YOUR TAURUS

Some people might call you stubborn, but you simply know what you believe in, and that is rare these days. You are headstrong, and you have faith in your mind and your emotions. Don't let anyone tell you how to think or feel. You're extremely intelligent, you are strong, and when you trust yourself you are unstoppable. Keep pushing yourself to make all of those beautiful dreams a reality.

GEMINI

Ⅱ

DATES May 21 - June 21

SIGN Twins

RULING PLANET Mercury

ZODIAC QUALITY Mutable

ELEMENT Air

POSITIVE TRAITS Friendly, Curious, Happy

NEGATIVE TRAITS Fickle, Flaky, Not Dependable

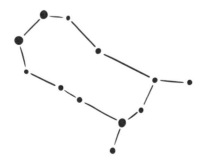

IF GEMINI WAS...

A STARBUCKS DRINK:
Salted Caramel Mocha

A COLOR:
Baby Blue

A GREEK GOD:
Athena—goddess of intelligence, skill, peace, and warfare

AN ADDICTION:
Smoking

AN ALCOHOLIC BEVERAGE:
Beer

A DRUG:
Salvia

IN A HIGH-SCHOOL CLIQUE:
Debate Club Kids

A CITY:
Tokyo, Japan

A HARRY POTTER HOUSE:
Gryffindor

AN UNTRANSLATABLE FRENCH WORD:
Épater—to wow, to stun, to amaze!

A KISS:
Playful

A TEEN MOVIE:
Bring It On

A CLOTHING ITEM:
Summer Dress

A FAMOUS LANDMARK:
The Colosseum

A SEASON:
Spring

GEMINI

PERSONALITY TRAITS

GEMINIS ARE OFTEN STRIVING to integrate socially while also striving to break away from societal authority. Despite being very outspoken, they are not the most rebellious sign. They simply revel in their individuality and value their personal freedom above everything else. When they need to be around others, they will make that happen; when they need to get away, they will cater to that. They live through both extremes. Geminis are very excitable when it comes to change, because they tend to bore easily. They will always prefer to search for excitement rather than stay home on a weekend and enjoy simple pleasures.

Geminis absolutely love going out and looking for trouble to get in with a pair of really good friends. To them, trouble means adventure and daring innovation. They believe searching for a little excitement will lead to a lot of fun, and they have many amazing stories to recount when they reveal the escapades to others who were unable to join them.

Geminis are full of nervous energy and are always trying to burn it off. Therefore, they are attracted to activities that produce a sense of exaltation within them. If they could fly, they would. Instead, Geminis focus on travel, and many forms of travel appeal to them. They love bikes, skates, cars, and motorcycles, though they get bored of long road trips. Geminis need a constant change of pace and direction.

Geminis are known to be the diversifier in its group of friends. They liven up every social situation with their vibrant personality and their flow of ideas. However, their leadership comes with absolutely no accepted responsibility or obligation or loyalty to the group with whom they choose to spend their time. Geminis are very nonattached creatures and will always go where the fun is.

GEMINI

COMPATIBILITY & RELATIONSHIPS

GEMINIS ARE THOUGHTFUL, VERY CHARMING, compelling, and quite dreamy. They need a match who is as deep as they are, someone who will cater to their love of knowledge and conversation. They like free thinkers and people who respect them. Aquarians will not be afraid of meeting them in their depths while stimulating the dreamy conversation and an insightful lifestyle. Together, Gemini and Aquarius would thrive as a true meeting of the minds.

GEMINI AND ARIES COMPATIBILITY: Aries and Gemini make an exciting couple that is always out of the house doing something fun together. They are the opposite of the "Netflix + Chill" homebody couple. Their Instagram feed makes most people exhausted, but they love living an active, adventurous life together.

GEMINI AND TAURUS COMPATIBILITY: Tauruses prize loyalty and stability above all else, which feels stifling to any Gemini they date. Similarly, Tauruses find Gemini's ways chaotic and unpredictable. These signs stress each other out!

GEMINI AND GEMINI COMPATIBILITY: If there was a "most likely to end up stranded in a foreign country" superlative for zodiac couples, the Gemini + Gemini pairing would get it. Their relationship will have problems, but all from the outside as they work to navigate the practical world as people who aren't detail-oriented. Their actual relationship, however, will be full of happiness and excitement—they'll love being unencumbered and totally themselves with someone who (finally) isn't trying to rein them in.

GEMINI AND CANCER COMPATIBILITY: Cancers primarily value their home life and the foundation of support they build with their partner, while Geminis thrive on *not* needing a foundation (which means they'd be stuck in one place for way too long). This sets up an uphill battle for couples because they aren't a natural pairing; however, this can make it all the more special when it *does* work.

GEMINI AND LEO COMPATIBILITY: Gemini and Leo are the couple you know who have the most fun together. They are always making big plans and making each other laugh. The little things will fall through the cracks, as neither person in this pairing is great at "adulting," but they'll be having too much fun to notice.

GEMINI AND VIRGO COMPATIBILITY: These two will drive each other CRAZY. Gemini will feel like a child to Virgo, and Virgo will feel like an overbearing parent to Gemini. Their friendship and romantic compatibility are almost zero.

GEMINI AND LIBRA COMPATIBILITY: These two make great friends and exciting and happy lovers. They are naturally compatible and like to spend their time the same way (around people, having fun). They are a social couple whom other couples aspire to be like.

GEMINI AND SCORPIO COMPATIBILITY: This pair is almost so alike that they don't work. They each can be stubborn and cold. They never think they are wrong and struggle in owning up to it when they are. Their fights are always very intense. They each have an acid tongue and tend to say things they later regret.

GEMINI AND SAGITTARIUS COMPATIBILITY: This pair will fall very hard for each other. It's the love they each remember in their lives, though it may end when Sagittarius begins to rely too much on Gemini and Gemini feels exhausted by the amount of emotional "homework" they feel they have to do. They walk away still with a lot of respect for each other.

GEMINI AND CAPRICORN COMPATIBILITY: This couple can make it work even though they aren't naturally compatible. Gemini can draw Capricorn out of their conservative shell, and Capricorn can provide the structure Gemini needs to truly thrive. As long as they are patient with each other and their differences, they can make a great couple.

GEMINI AND AQUARIUS COMPATIBILITY: These two make better friends than lovers, but they get along swimmingly. They are both exciting people who love to explore new ideas. They have nonstop conversation and keep each other interested in what can be a very passionate relationship.

GEMINI AND PISCES COMPATIBILITY: Gemini + Pisces balance each other out very well. While Pisces are very emotional and deep, Geminis are very compassionate and understanding of their needs. Pisces have no shame in being exactly who they are, which gains them a lot of respect from Gemini. Together, they can have a fun, expression-filled relationship.

HOW TO ATTRACT GEMINI

If you want to attract Gemini, dress to impress. They love a sharp fashion sense and are always checking out those who take care of themselves physically. Their own physical appearance says a lot about them, so they are often attracted to a partner that cares just as much about what image they are projecting.

HOW TO KNOW IF GEMINI LIKES YOU

If Gemini likes you, they will not stop talking to you. They will ask questions, make conversation, and keep the momentum going. It is often said that Gemini tells you that they like you with their eyes—they will be absorbed by you and will stare deeply at you. Though they will try to play it cool, if Geminis are paying more attention to you than others, you can be sure that they like you. They usually don't waste time with people who do not intrigue them. They will be touchy and will often whisk you off of your feet when you least expect it. However, you must be wary of Gemini. They are known players, often leading people on for the sheer fun and adventure of it.

HOW GEMINIS ARE IN A RELATIONSHIP

Dating Geminis is a thrilling experience. They are full of fun and always up for learning and gaining the most out of every situation. They are natural-born flirts, and the banter with them will keep you on your toes and laughing for the duration of your relationship. However, when they do choose you, know that they have chosen you for a reason. Gemini do not get into a relationship until they have met their match intellectually and energetically. They have had plenty of practice, and they are known to get around, so when they do settle down, they are very self-assured and absolutely compelled by their choice. To stay happy in a relationship, Geminis need change, stimulation, and excitement. If you can give that to them, they will be yours for life.

GEMINI'S IDEAL DATE

Geminis are thirsty for knowledge. They always want to learn new things. An ideal date would stimulate this aspect of their personality. Take them out to watch the premiere of a new documentary, and then go for drinks so you can chat about everything you noticed and absorbed from the film. They will be stimulated the whole night.

HOW GEMINIS ARE IN THE BEDROOM

Geminis will always shake it up in the bedroom. You will never know what is coming next. They adore having their arms and their thighs touched. They are all over the place in regards to their sexual style, ranging from making love to you to being absolute filthy animals underneath the sheets. Expect an adventure if you choose to sleep with Gemini.

HOW GEMINIS DEAL WITH HEARTBREAK

Geminis will act like they do not care when their heart is broken. They will never take on any responsibility for ending the companionship and will always blame the other person for being unworthy and ill-equipped. This stems from their extremely superficial and prideful personality. They will likely set out to find someone better for them, searching for the next upgrade they can sink their teeth into instead of coping emotionally.

HOW GEMINIS ARE AS FRIENDS

Geminis are often considered to be the social connector in the group. They bring together a lot of different people, merging different friendship cliques and creating inclusive companionships. Whenever Geminis are around, there will always be laughter and fun. However, Gemini can be an extremely flaky friend, and they will never commit to a plan because they are always worried that something better will come up. Though they have large circles of friends, if Gemini calls you their best friend, you can be sure that you are one of the very few close people in their life.

HOW TO GAIN THE RESPECT OF GEMINI

Gemini will respect you if you are well-spoken, well-dressed, and if you are witty. They appreciate banter and think that those who can dish it out are intelligent and superior to those who can't.

HOW GEMINIS ARE WHEN THEY'RE MAD

Geminis are the most talkative sign in the zodiac, so it comes as no surprise that they tend to get mad and unleash their anger in the form of screaming, shouting, and cursing. They know how to break someone down using words, and they will not hesitate to do so. When you get the other side of an angry Gemini, they can be level-headed and calm, using extremely mean and cutting language to passively hurt you. They always go right for the jugular. If you judge Gemini or if you tell them what to do, expect to get verbally assaulted.

HOW GEMINIS ARE WHEN THEY'RE SAD

When sad, Geminis get very quiet. However, inside their mind is racing as they consume themselves in a bout of overthinking. They absolutely hate being sad and refuse to allow themselves to feel morose, often disassociating and detaching to forget about their sensitivities.

SIMPLE THINGS THAT MAKE GEMINIS HAPPY

It's quite simple—Geminis are happy when they are validated, especially on an emotional level. They love knowing that their input is appreciated.

GEMINIS AT THEIR BEST

At their best, Geminis are strongly adaptable and resourceful. They are always good at what they put their mind to, and they are ridiculously intelligent. They are so much fun, and they inspire people to live their lives to the fullest.

GEMINIS AT THEIR WORST

At their worst, Geminis are often all over the place. They can be scatterbrained and often won't correct themselves if they make mistakes. They will never apologize and will shout if someone calls them out for being a little hardened to judgment.

WHAT GEMINIS FEAR THE MOST

The main facet of any Gemini's personality is expressiveness. Therefore, they often fear not being able to express themselves fully. They are scared that they will be blocked from following their passions. They often worry that they aren't as talented or intelligent as they think they are.

GEMINI'S LIKELY OCCUPATIONS

Geminis love intellectual, stimulating work. They work best in fast-paced, high-pressure environments where they will be required to work on many different things. A job that requires Gemini to travel or network will be perfect for the constantly adventuring and social twin. They would make great stockbrokers, architects, and teachers.

GEMINI'S LIKELY HEALTH CONCERNS

The Gemini in your life is ruled by their lungs and their respiratory system. When working the way they do, Geminis must slow down and nurture their body, because they can often deplete their energy and suffer from collapsed lungs, colds, bronchitis, and asthma. Meditation is the best form of preventive medicine for Gemini, for it relaxes them and allows them to reconnect with their breathing.

WHERE TO TAKE GEMINIS ON VACATION

Geminis love to roam freely, and they need a lot of stimulation from the places they decide to explore. Big cities appeal to them, and a place like London is an amazing fit for Gemini because they would have an array of options from which to choose. They can drink all they want, explore museums, look at incredible landmarks, order room service from a swanky hotel, or simply take in the city's beautifully vibrant nature.

GEMINI'S LEARNING STYLE

Geminis need to talk about anything they are learning. Whether it is talking through a lecture or talking about something they saw in a movie that they want to figure out in their brain, they need to be able to think out loud. Verbally repeating information and sharing that conversation with others who can challenge them with questions and stimulate their knowledge is the best way for Gemini to learn.

GEMINI'S HUMOR

Quick on the uptake, they remember jokes really well and can laugh at just about anything. This sign is most prone to making fun of someone, but not in a mean way; it's usually because they're interested.

GEMINI'S FAVORITE PASTIME

Talking. Literally, just talking.

WHAT TO SAY TO MOTIVATE YOUR GEMINI

You are filled with fire—do not let anyone put that out inside of you. You have the capacity to make everyone around you laugh, you are interesting, and you have an incredible energy to you. You are the epitome of fascinating.

CANCER

DATES	June 21 – July 22
SIGN	Crab
RULING PLANET	Moon
ZODIAC QUALITY	Cardinal
ELEMENT	Water
POSITIVE TRAITS	Nurturing, Loving, Creative
NEGATIVE TRAITS	Moody, Snobby, Overly Sensitive

IF CANCER WAS...

A STARBUCKS DRINK:
Hazelnut Chai

A COLOR:
Lilac

A GREEK GOD:
Eros—god of love and sex

AN ADDICTION:
Another Human Being

AN ALCOHOLIC BEVERAGE:
Margarita

A DRUG:
LSD

IN A HIGH-SCHOOL CLIQUE:
Poets / Loners

A CITY:
Amsterdam, Holland

A HARRY POTTER HOUSE:
Hufflepuff

AN UNTRANSLATABLE FRENCH WORD:
Flâner—wandering the streets of Paris with no goal,
only to enjoy the beauty of the city

A KISS:
Gentle

A TEEN MOVIE:
Hairspray

A CLOTHING ITEM:
A Fuzzy Sweater

A FAMOUS LANDMARK:
The Amazon River

A SEASON:
Winter

CANCER

PERSONALITY TRAITS

CANCERS ARE KNOWN TO BE DOMESTICATED BEINGS. They represent deep feeling and protectiveness. Cancers are also associated with highly personal emotions and dreamlike foundations. However, they often hide their depths in order to guard their hearts.

Cancers are protective and sensitive, yes, but they are also very aggressive and strong-willed when it comes to getting what they want. They prefer to avoid making demands and expect others to understand their needs, moods, and varying feelings.

Cancers really admire those they with whom they can create a tight-knit, compassionate bond. They crave deep and emotional friendship, and they dedicate themselves to sharing as much as they can with someone when they do find such a match. On the other hand, they find it difficult and hard to open up to those who do not personally understand them and often won't bother trying to befriend or court them.

Cancers are very unusual, but they are also extremely self-aware. They know that they are different, and they know why. They love eating, sleeping, expressing themselves sexually, and sympathizing, but it all must be done behind closed doors. They are private people who need those things in very large doses to feel supported and nurtured. Without all of those things listed above, Cancers will often succumb to feelings of nervousness and irritability.

CANCER

COMPATIBILITY & RELATIONSHIPS

CANCERS ARE SENSITIVE, NURTURING, affectionate, and dependent. They need someone who will cater to their homebody lifestyle, and they seek a mate who will be like family to them. They want to adore someone, but they need that in return as well. Any imbalance and Cancer will feel threatened and misunderstood. Taurus would be best for Cancer, for they both love to indulge and nest while still being highly intuitive and deep.

CANCER AND ARIES COMPATIBILITY: This is a difficult relationship, as Aries will always feel slowed down by their Cancer, and Cancer will always feel like they can't relax around Aries. They have different values and different dispositions—and not necessarily in a complementary way. However, with the right people this relationship can work—Aries will inject excitement into Cancer's life and draw them out of their shell, and Cancer will help Aries venture into their own minds and get in touch with their emotional needs.

CANCER AND TAURUS COMPATIBILITY: This has the potential to be one of the best matches in the zodiac. Taurus and Cancer are similar people with complementary values. They will enjoy building a happy home life together, having an extremely loyal and supportive partner, and spoiling each other with physical touch, comforting meals, and endless affection.

CANCER AND GEMINI COMPATIBILITY: Cancers primarily value their home life and the foundation of support they build with their partner, while Geminis thrive on *not* needing a foundation (which means they'd be stuck in one place for way too long). This sets up an uphill battle for couples because they aren't a natural pairing—HOWEVER—this can make it all the more special when it *does* work.

CANCER AND CANCER COMPATIBILITY: Cancer + Cancer is a heavy match. The two will get along amazingly and are capable of having one of the deepest relationships in the zodiac because they understand each other so well. The only problem with this relationship is that there are times where it might feel *too* deep, with no one to lighten up the intensity. Both partners will feel like they need to come up for air at times.

CANCER AND LEO COMPATIBILITY: Cancers won't immediately enjoy playing second fiddle to Leo—not because they crave the spotlight for themselves, but because they view Leo's vain ways as inauthentic or even shallow. This is a small problem in the grand scheme of life and relationships and one that's easily gotten over once you know someone well. There's potential for real balance here, as the signs are different enough that they can truly support and complement each other.

CANCER AND VIRGO COMPATIBILITY: There's a lot of potential for harmony in Cancer + Virgo, as both signs seek to avoid conflict and take great pains to make sure their partner feels happy and supported. What they lack in natural chemistry, they more than make up for in effort—this pairing is one of two active, communicative people who will put their relationship first.

CANCER AND LIBRA COMPATIBILITY: Cancer and Libra will get along well, and their biggest fight will just be about whether to stay in or go out with friends. There's no big chemistry fireworks here, but that often just means less drama and more harmony.

CANCER AND SCORPIO COMPATIBILITY: Many believe this is the best match in the entire zodiac. These two signs understand and complement each other perfectly, even though on the surface they tend to have different personalities. What works here is that each person in the relationship is strong where the other is weak. They're both very interested in having a strong relationship (something they're willing to put work into), and they have similar goals in life they're going to want to work together to achieve.

CANCER AND SAGITTARIUS COMPATIBILITY: It's hard to see why these two signs would get together, as they don't have similar values or personalities—but they also are both laid-back and like to avoid conflict, so they don't fight a lot as a couple. With the right two people, this could be an easy relationship celebrating the lighter side of Cancer and the deeper side of Sag.

CANCER AND CAPRICORN COMPATIBILITY: It will be a bit of a struggle for these two to align their values, but they're not totally incompatible. Capricorn will seem a bit shallow to Cancer until they explain that they like nice things because it creates a relaxing home environment (among other things). That's a goal they are happy to work toward together, and Capricorn will appreciate how loyal Cancer is. Both will prize the relationship above all else.

CANCER AND AQUARIUS COMPATIBILITY: On paper this pairing should do well, but it often feels like something here won't "click." These two people understand each other's needs, but they don't move naturally together. Aquarius will seem too removed from their body and emotions to Cancer, and Cancer will seem too needy and emotional for Aquarius.

CANCER AND PISCES COMPATIBILITY: Cancer and Pisces will fundamentally understand each other, but they're so similar that they will have a hard time functioning in the real world as a couple. Both of these signs work best when they're paired with a sturdier person who lives in the real world—not another dreamer. This point aside, they will be perfectly happy together and will create a beautiful, creative world where everyone is nice to each other.

HOW TO ATTRACT CANCERS

To attract Cancer, make sure that you smile at them. They absolutely adore genuine, kind grins and it will show them that you are approachable. By being open to Cancer, you show them that you are caring, and this is a trait that is simply irresistible in their eyes.

HOW TO KNOW IF CANCER LIKES YOU

Cancers are very shy and very sweet when they like someone. Though they may not show it, you can always tell if Cancer likes you by observing how their friends act around you. Cancer will tell everyone they are close to about the apple of their eye, and their loyal friends will help to get you two together. If you catch Cancer looking at you, they are probably contemplating how to approach you and how to interact with you, as everything about them is coy and cautious. Be open to them if you feel like getting to know them as well, for this cautiousness comes from a deeply insecure fear of rejection.

HOW CANCERS ARE IN A RELATIONSHIP

Cancers are unbelievably tender and gentle. They are kind souls that feel deeply and all too much. They are considered the most sensitive sign in the zodiac, and they won't hesitate to show that to their significant other. When committed, Cancer will never second-guess the person they are with, and they will pour oceans of love into them. They seek a mate who can understand them, so their relationships are often very emotional, intuitive partnerships that are devoted and lifelong.

CANCER'S IDEAL DATE

Cancers love to feel comfortable and often go out to familiar places when they venture into the public eye. An ideal date would be one that brings Cancer somewhere they have already been, like their favorite restaurant. They will find the gesture thoughtful, and they will open up and really shine in the safe environment.

HOW CANCERS ARE IN THE BEDROOM

Cancers are known to be submissive in bed, allowing for their partners to fully explore their body and do whatever they please. However, Cancers do love rough talk and will harmonize the bedroom session with tender kisses and gentle caresses. With Cancer, you are getting the best of both worlds.

HOW CANCERS DEAL WITH HEARTBREAK

Because they are often hurt, Cancers take a long time to open up and trust someone. Therefore, if they have their heart broken by someone they genuinely thought they could confide in and love, they will take the breakup very badly. Cancers tend to always look into their past, and they drive themselves crazy overanalyzing what went wrong and how they could have changed or prevented the outcome. It will always take a long time for Cancer to move on.

HOW CANCERS ARE AS FRIENDS

If you are lucky enough to have Cancer in your friend group, you know that they tend to be the protectors. They consider their friends to be their family, and they cherish every moment with them. They hold every memory close to their heart, and they give everything they have to make their friendships strong. Cancers, however, believe that friendships are two-way streets. Therefore, they need to see effort and appreciation on the other side of the fence as well, or else they will feel used and hurt.

HOW TO GAIN THE RESPECT OF CANCERS

Cancers always respect those who have good reputations. They are impressed by people who prove that they can be trusted, and they often appreciate those who are endearing.

HOW CANCERS ARE WHEN THEY'RE MAD

When mad, Cancers will start sulking loudly. If no one catches on to that, they will move on to passive manners before turning to isolation. However, instead of leaving them alone when they go into isolation, in those moments

Cancers need to know that they are noticed and cared for. If a friend does not express to them that they are appreciated, or if someone is mean to them during this period, they will start hysterically crying. They build their emotions up inside of them until they bubble over, causing every pent-up feeling and sensitivity to result in waterworks.

HOW CANCERS ARE WHEN THEY'RE SAD

When sad, Cancers will again start to cry. They will isolate themselves and the separation will feel so severe it will manifest into stomachaches and headaches. Because Cancers feel so much, being sad is difficult, but it comes very easy to them. They are very quick to break down.

SIMPLE THINGS THAT MAKE CANCERS HAPPY

When Cancers need alone time and they get it, they are extremely thrilled. They also love cuddling and being wrapped up in the arms of someone they care deeply about.

CANCERS AT THEIR BEST

At their best, Cancers are hardworking, deeply sensitive people. They try to protect every heart they encounter, and they act like a nurturing force in so many lives. It is rare to find someone who cares as much as Cancer, and it is their best attribute.

CANCERS AT THEIR WORST

At their worst, Cancers tend to butt into matters that don't really concern them. They can be very judgmental and guarded, while their need to protect themselves allows for them to come off in a "holier than thou" light.

WHAT CANCERS FEAR THE MOST

Cancers deeply fear rejection. Due to having so many feelings and being so sensitive, Cancers have a large capacity to love. They fear never being able to find someone who can handle all of what they have to offer, and they can be unwilling to offer up their heart for fear of it being turned down. Cancers carry the wound of rejection far longer than most.

CANCER'S LIKELY OCCUPATIONS

As nurturers, Cancers would work best in an area of employment that caters to their sensitivity and compassion. They give amazing advice and are very protective while still being responsible problem-solvers. Cancer would make an amazing social worker, a brilliant teacher, and a very compassionate CEO.

CANCER'S LIKELY HEALTH CONCERNS

Cancers are ruled by the gut and the stomach. Therefore, Cancers have to watch their extremely strong emotions, for they tend to cause acid reflux and fluid buildup in their guts. They suffer from stomachaches when upset as well. Cancers must focus on being calm and truly just going with the flow of their emotions rather than allowing them to escalate into uncontrollable storms.

WHERE TO TAKE CANCERS ON VACATION

Cancers are homebodies, so their ideal vacation often includes something comforting. This doesn't mean that Cancers can't travel, however. Cancers will always feel energized and safe around water, and a bed and breakfast (versus a large hotel) would make their vacation feel just like home.

CANCER'S LEARNING STYLE

Cancers learn best in an environment that nurtures them. Working from home would be an amazing way to gain knowledge for Cancers, especially if it involved studying from bed.

CANCER'S HUMOR

Often self-deprecating, Cancers have an odd way of being funny. They tend to make fun of themselves in order to stay guarded and can usually be found making silly facial expressions to get a quick laugh.

CANCER'S FAVORITE PASTIMES

Cancers thoroughly enjoy reading, fashion, and cooking.

WHAT TO SAY TO MOTIVATE YOUR CANCER

The way you feel your emotions is incredible. You are in touch with every facet of your heart and its sensitivity. Your ability to believe in others and to trust that we all hold good within us is beautiful. Don't let anyone tell you that your vulnerability is a bad thing. Don't let your heart harden. Don't let the world jade you. Keep feeling, keep having faith in others. The right people know that you are a rare gem in this world.

L Ɛ O

DATES	July 22 – August 23
SIGN	Lion
RULING PLANET	Sun
ZODIAC QUALITY	Fixed
ELEMENT	Fire
POSITIVE TRAITS	Confident, Entertaining, Creative
NEGATIVE TRAITS	Self-Centered, Bragging, Unsympathetic

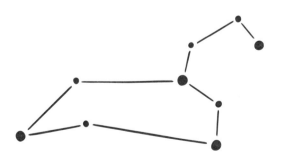

IF LEO WAS...

A STARBUCKS DRINK:
Pumpkin Spice Latte

A COLOR:
Gold

A GREEK GOD:
Apollo—God of music, arts, healing, and the sun

AN ADDICTION:
Shopping

AN ALCOHOLIC BEVERAGE:
Champagne

A DRUG:
Cocaine

IN A HIGH-SCHOOL CLIQUE:
Drama Club Kids

A CITY:
Hollywood, California

A HARRY POTTER HOUSE:
Gryffindor

AN UNTRANSLATABLE FRENCH PHRASE:
La douleur exquise—the pain of unrequited love

A KISS:
Heated

A TEEN MOVIE:
Clueless

A CLOTHING ITEM:
Anything Sparkly

A FAMOUS LANDMARK:
Versailles

A SEASON:
Summer

LEO

PERSONALITY TRAITS

LEOS ARE RADIANT, CREATIVE FORCES that light up the zodiac. They have a powerful energy under control. Those born under this sign symbolize the need of the ego and its necessity in making the world a better place. Ambition, self-confidence and power are the cornerstones of this sign, and they are almost always very well respected by their peers.

Leos have fully realized their expression through direct action. They are leaders, and they expect others to follow them without question. The great thing about Leos is that their ego does not harden them to others. They gain followers easily because they still have a warmth to them, and they are very sunny in nature. They are harmonized individuals who have a lot to teach those who will listen.

Leos are considered very mature and self-assured. They know exactly what they bring to the table and aren't afraid of making their presence felt through grand gestures. However, despite their popularity, Leos hate pettiness and meanness, and they often overlook those who engage in such immature antics. Leos are big-hearted, and they give everything to their goals and what they are trying to achieve.

Leos are also extremely honorable and will always stick to their word. They will pay off bets they have lost, and they will say no to advances that do not match up with their wants. Leos think about their opportunities and don't just take everything that is handed to them.

To Leos, a lot of pride is found in where they live. They need to reside in a castle-like environment where they can entertain and share their hospitality with others. They are loyal and faithful and will defend someone until they are blue in the face. This fixed attitude can cause a lot of problems for Leos, because they can be wrong sometimes, and they often refuse to admit that.

LEO

COMPATIBILITY & RELATIONSHIPS

LEOS ARE IDEALISTIC, sometimes insecure, and quite affectionate. They work best with someone who will love them during their good times and their bad times. They need someone who will appreciate their wins and help them to navigate their losses. Leos need independence, but they also need security. A fun-loving Sagittarius would be perfect for Leo, because they would complement the Lion's need for adventure while meeting their need for stimulation both emotionally and physically.

LEO AND ARIES COMPATIBILITY: Aries and Leo are natural allies and make great friends. They love to try new things together, go on adventures, be silly, and challenge themselves. As a couple, they'd have the most jealousy-inducing Instagram of all time.

LEO AND TAURUS COMPATIBILITY: Jealousy will be a big problem in this relationship, as Taurus will never be comfortable with Leo's constant need for attention. As a result, insecure Taurus will never feel like they are able to completely relax, while Leo will feel like they are constantly walking on eggshells.

LEO AND GEMINI COMPATIBILITY: Gemini and Leo are the couple you know who have the most fun together. They are always making big plans and making each other laugh. The little things will fall through the cracks, as neither person in this pairing is great at "adulting," but they'll be having too much fun to notice.

LEO AND CANCER COMPATIBILITY: Cancer won't immediately enjoy playing second fiddle to Leo; not because they crave the spotlight for themselves but because they view Leo's vain ways as inauthentic or even shallow. This is a small problem in the grand scheme of life and relationships and one that's easily gotten over once you know someone well. There's potential for real balance here, as the signs are different enough that they can truly support and complement each other.

LEO AND LEO COMPATIBILITY: The biggest problem for Leos dating another Leo is that they both want to be the star. It will be hard for them to find balance as a couple and make sure both people's needs are being met.

LEO AND VIRGO COMPATIBILITY: Leo and Virgo can have a happy, harmonious relationship if they are emotionally mature and the kind of people who can appreciate someone's different strengths and weaknesses rather than expecting their partner to be exactly like them. Virgo will be happy to let Leo be the star, and Leo will love how Virgo is totally comfortable being out of the spotlight. Together they balance each other out and truly support each other's hopes and dreams.

LEO AND LIBRA COMPATIBILITY: Leo and Libra both love the spotlight, but somehow they aren't competitive with each other about it. They'd rather share it (rare for both signs) and let the light shine on how happy they make each other as a couple.

LEO AND SCORPIO COMPATIBILITY: In a relationship, Leos need to be in the spotlight, and Scorpio does not let them have it automatically. While Scorpio knows when to fight their battles and chooses them wisely, the biggest issue this pair has is a fight for power in the relationship.

LEO AND SAGITTARIUS COMPATIBILITY: This is a fun-loving couple that gets along well and typically has zero drama. They understand and appreciate each other's nature and would rather spend time doing instead of talking. They tend to be a busy couple who don't spend a lot of time at home.

LEO AND CAPRICORN COMPATIBILITY: An unlikely pairing, but one that can create a really strong couple. Leo and Capricorn both love being respected and appreciated by their peers and will work together to guard their privacy and make sure their reputations are what they desire. Neither is too wild, and while Capricorns can be prudish, that generally ends behind closed doors, which is all that matters to Leo.

LEO AND AQUARIUS COMPATIBILITY: Leo and Aquarius get along best in the bedroom where they are drawn to an exciting, non-vanilla relationship. Outside the bedroom, they have less in common, but if they put work into really getting to know each other, they can form a strong bond as a couple.

LEO AND PISCES COMPATIBILITY: In this relationship Leo has to be the strong and stable one. Pisces are very needy in relationships. Because everything in Pisces's life is based on how they feel, they need a partner who understands and can nurture them. Where Pisces might lack confidence, Leo has it in spades. Where Pisces might crumble, Leo has no problem being their strength. This couple is good together when each person understands the role they play, but problems occur most the time when being the adult one becomes too much for Leo.

HOW TO ATTRACT LEO

Leo will be instantly attracted to you if you bring attention to them. It will prove to them that you are mindful of them, and it will cater to their unceasing need for popularity and affirmation. Leo always loves to be looked up to, so if you casually compliment them while in the middle of a conversation or in front of a group of people, you will stroke their ego and find your way right into their heart.

HOW TO KNOW IF LEO LIKES YOU

In all honesty, Leo will most likely just tell you that they are fond of you. Everyone will know that Leo likes you because they do not back down from those they are interested in and will declare their affection. They will play games and they will also get very touchy, so if Leo keeps grabbing you, tickling you, or smiling at you from across the room, they are definitely fond of you. If Leo really likes you, they will pay more attention to you with their eye contact, and they won't break it. They will also talk to you differently than others, using a sweeter, smoother tone. They will always try to impress you—be sure not to see this as arrogance, because it is simply nervous flirting.

HOW LEOS ARE IN A RELATIONSHIP

In a relationship, Leos tend to be very passionate. Their fiery nature will heat things up with affection and adventure. They choose their mates based on their ability to be dominant in a relationship, so they will often be the leader out of the two partners. In a relationship, Leo needs to be the center of attention, as he or she believes that they deserve to shine the brightest in any situation. Generous and giving, Leo will create a wonderful life for the apple of their eye but must always be nurtured because they tend to get insecure from time to time.

IDEAL DATE FOR LEOS

Leo loves having every eye on them when they are in a room. Bring them to karaoke and watch them get up onstage and put on a show for the world to see. Leos will love to see you in the crowd, cheering them on and taking in how fun they are.

HOW LEOS ARE IN THE BEDROOM

Though Leos tend to be very dominant in the public eye, in the bedroom they are usually a mix between a top and a bottom. Whatever their partner likes is what Leo will dish out. They love to look into the eyes of the person they are sleeping with and are very sensual in that sense, as they take sex seriously. They adore having their back scratched, and they will more than likely bite your lip in the act.

HOW LEOS DEAL WITH HEARTBREAK

Just like a lion, Leo revels in their pride. Therefore, to have their heart broken rather than to break the heart of the person they were with often hurts their ego. Leo, however, will hide that bruised ego and they will hold their head up high—moving on in a very regal and poised manner. They will go searching for attention and affection as a means of healing and recharging their ego.

HOW LEOS ARE AS FRIENDS

Having Leo as a best friend is a lot of fun. They are generous and adored by so many people. They love having the spotlight on them and are often considered bossy. However, a lot of people will turn a blind eye to how bossy Leo is because they are so fun. They always know how to cheer people up, and everyone wants to keep the lion around because of its good nature and thrilling personality.

HOW TO GAIN LEO'S RESPECT

To impress Leo is simple. Demand attention, be charming, and look them straight in the eye. They respect anyone who challenges them. Just don't steal their spotlight.

HOW LEOS ARE WHEN THEY'RE MAD

When mad, the lion goes beyond anger and often fills with red-hot rage. Their roar is louder than any other sign in the zodiac, and they can often be found intensely shouting to feel better. They are crude, often resorting to using offensive language and blowing up on people who do not deserve it. However, they will never apologize when they are in the wrong, because their ego will never allow them.

HOW LEOS ARE WHEN THEY'RE SAD

When sad, Leos get very wound-up. They fester in their emotions and build them up to the point where they unravel and have a nervous breakdown. They are extremely short-tempered when sad, though they are also extremely needy. Those closest to them know how to help, though they are at risk for being hurt due to Leo's tendency to blow up when sad.

SIMPLE THINGS THAT MAKE LEOS HAPPY

Leos absolutely love being around people. For attention-seeking Leos, the presence of others allows them to shine, therefore they feel happiest when they have an audience. They also enjoy watching their favorite shows with someone they love.

LEOS AT THEIR BEST

At their best, the courageous Leo is strong and has an amazing, protective attitude toward their friends. They care very deeply for those close to them. Leo is the bravest sign in the zodiac, often doing whatever they are required to do despite being scared or in danger. They are thoughtful, kind, and generous, and this is why they are so well-liked.

LEOS AT THEIR WORST

At their worst, Leos are overly excitable, and they hang around with the wrong people, as it hard to know who your real friends are when you have such a large group of people who want a piece of you. They are bad listeners, and they cannot apologize for being wrong when they are very clearly at fault.

WHAT LEOS FEAR THE MOST

Though Leos present to the world this idea of a fearless leader, the lion fears that it will be undervalued and underappreciated. The fear of being unnoticed runs very deep in Leos, and their insecurity sometimes knocks them right off their feet.

LIKELY OCCUPATIONS FOR LEOS

Leos are natural-born leaders. They are fearless and independent and work best when they are in the spotlight. They admire jobs that bring them status and power, as they cannot work when they are boxed-in and required to follow someone else's lead. Due to their spontaneity and sheer charm, Leos would make amazing CEOs. They would also excel in real estate, design, and politics.

LIKELY HEALTH CONCERNS FOR LEOS

Leos are ruled by the sun, the center of everything. Therefore, Leos are prone to ailments that relate to their heart and their spine. Leo must get a lot of exercise to combat the long work days they often put themselves through, and they will need to learn how to recharge their spirit to avoid any medical problems.

WHERE TO TAKE LEOS ON VACATION

Leos always need to be in the center of the action. They want to be stimulated with good parties and prospective adventures. They will thrive somewhere hip that has bars and thrill-seeking activities. Being able to drink and dance all night and zipline during the day will make Leo feel like they aren't compromising any facet of their personality or missing out on anything while traveling.

LEOS' LEARNING STYLE

Leos will learn best in a one-on-one environment. This will allow them to show off their knowledge and bask in the teacher's attention.

LEOS' HUMOR

Leos will hook you with their humor, and they know it. They have the ability to take in everything around them and serve funny jokes about those things seamlessly. They will use exaggeration to make people chuckle, and groups will often be found laughing loudly in their presence.

FAVORITE PASTIME FOR LEOS

Leos love to draw, watch funny TV shows, and they will never say no to doing something reckless or impossible.

WHAT TO SAY TO MOTIVATE YOUR LEO

You hold within you this charisma that stops people in their tracks. You are charming, interesting, and captivate everyone around you. When you speak, people listen. When you walk into a room, everyone stares. You capture people. You will always get what you want, so don't forget that this also applies to your dreams. Ask for what you need, and take it when it comes to you. Push doors open. Nothing can tie you down.

VIRGO

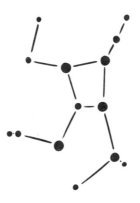

DATES	August 23 – September 23
SIGN	Virgin
RULING PLANET	Mercury
ZODIAC QUALITY	Mutable
ELEMENT	Earth
POSITIVE TRAITS	Ambitious, Intelligent, Hard Worker
NEGATIVE TRAITS	Bossy, Aggressive, Judgmental

IF VIRGO WAS...

A STARBUCKS DRINK:
Espresso

A COLOR:
Beige

A GREEK GOD:
Attis—god of rebirth

AN ADDICTION:
Cleaning

AN ALCOHOLIC BEVERAGE:
White Wine

A DRUG:
Adderall

IN A HIGH-SCHOOL CLIQUE:
Nerds

A CITY:
Moscow, Russia

A HARRY POTTER HOUSE:
Slytherin

AN UNTRANSLATABLE FRENCH PHRASE:
Savoir-faire—knowing how to act appropriately in social situations

A KISS:
Soft

A TEEN MOVIE:
The Princess Diaries

A CLOTHING ITEM:
Freshly Ironed Shirt

A FAMOUS LANDMARK:
The Eiffel Tower

A SEASON:
Fall

VIRGO

PERSONALITY TRAITS

VIRGOS ARE KNOWN TO BE VERY ANALYTICAL, careful, and orderly. They represent a very uniform and systematic approach to life and problem-solving. They are known to ground others and are highly selective when it comes to human experience.

Virgos are very mature and secretive and often control exactly what they can reveal and exactly what they must bottle up inside of them. Their minds are not filled with dreams; rather, they are brimming with analysis and observation. Virgos are the kind of people who will plan ahead and focus on their goals. Whether it's saving up for a trip or asking for a promotion, Virgos will always have a few months of overanalyzing and methodology behind their decisions.

Virgos do, however, enjoy spontaneity and adventure. However, they need a little bit of structure if they are going to enjoy themselves. Virgos make great contributors and are amazing employees, family members, and caregivers.

Virgos tend to take things literally. Therefore, they are extremely loyal creatures. Their sense of humor is all over the place, sometimes being bogged down by how serious they get. Virgos will often make silent demands, thinking that those who understand them will simply pick up on their invisible cues and give them what they need. Modest and even prudish, Virgos love being in control of their lives.

VIRGO

COMPATIBILITY & RELATIONSHIPS

VIRGOS ARE VERY FOCUSED on perfection, and they are quite paranoid creatures. They need a partner who will give them the gentle, steady love that they crave and need to open up and flourish. A good match for Virgo will ease their worries, and they will appreciate and encourage how much Virgo cares about them. A great partner for practical Virgo would be Taurus, who also shares a tendency to be introverted while appreciating harmony and the exact kind of security Virgo offers.

VIRGO AND ARIES COMPATIBILITY: This is a natural pairing of two complementary people. Aries will pick the adventure, and Virgo will plan it out. They will challenge and balance each other and genuinely make the other person's life better.

VIRGO AND TAURUS COMPATIBILITY: What most people describe as "boring," this couple will describe as "ideal." They are on the same page about many things in life, from finances to where they want to be in five years. They will support each other and make each other feel fully confident in the relationship.

VIRGO AND GEMINI COMPATIBILITY: These two will drive each other CRAZY. Gemini will feel like a child to Virgo, and Virgo will feel like an overbearing parent to Gemini. Their friendship and romantic compatibility are almost zero.

VIRGO AND CANCER COMPATIBILITY: There's a lot of potential for harmony in Cancer + Virgo, as both signs seek to avoid conflict and take great pains to make sure their partner feels happy and supported. What they lack in natural chemistry, they more than make up for in effort—this pairing is one of two active, communicative people who will put their relationship first.

VIRGO AND LEO COMPATIBILITY: Leo and Virgo can have a happy, harmonious relationship if they are emotionally mature and the kind of people who can appreciate someone's different strengths and weaknesses rather than expecting their partner to be exactly like them. Virgo will be happy to let Leo be the star, and Leo will love how Virgo is totally comfortable being out of the spotlight. Together they balance each other out and truly support each other's hopes and dreams.

VIRGO AND VIRGO COMPATIBILITY: Virgo gets along well with another Virgo, but they'd do better with someone who complements them. With another Virgo, they tend to stick in their conservative little life instead of exploring the world or trying anything new. In the end, they may feel they have settled.

VIRGO AND LIBRA COMPATIBILITY: Virgo and Libra can be a stable couple that make each other perfectly happy. It might not all be vacations and fireworks, but they support each other and don't piss each other off. They both value harmony and don't like conflict for the sake of conflict. They'll be very good at communicating with each other and checking in to make sure they are both happy.

VIRGO AND SCORPIO COMPATIBILITY: This isn't the best combination there is, but it also isn't the worst. Together the strong parts of the relationship come out in the form of support. They each work hard and are motivated and driven. They each care a lot about being successful. The relationship isn't their number-one priority, but they respect that. While it's a healthy relationship, it's not the one that sends you head over heels.

VIRGO AND SAGITTARIUS COMPATIBILITY: This can be a good opposites-attract relationship, as their strengths and weaknesses are complementary, and they aren't so opposite that they will drive each other crazy. Sagittarius will force Virgo to have fun, and Virgo will make sure Sagittarius doesn't fall off a cliff somewhere.

VIRGO AND CAPRICORN COMPATIBILITY: This is a power couple in the making. Both people are ambitious, hardworking, and somewhat conservative when it comes to their personal lives. They will take a while to open up and be vulnerable with each other, but their interests are so in line that once that happens they'll be a perfect team.

VIRGO AND AQUARIUS COMPATIBILITY: Virgo is going to think Aquarius is a bit crazy at first, but in time they will find out they aren't so incompatible after all. Aquarius, for all their wacky ideas, isn't a total mess like Gemini and can take care of themselves. There'll be a little spark here as both people are somewhat foreign and exotic to the other.

VIRGO AND PISCES COMPATIBILITY: This combination is the relationship every parent wants their kids to be in. It's a practical relationship with a down-to-earth and productive duo. While it might not be that love story that keeps you up at night, they are the love you know will be loyal and people who will keep their vows if ever you choose each other.

HOW TO ATTRACT VIRGOS

To attract Virgos, you have to flirt with them. Try to make things with them fun and playful, both physically and through conversation. Work to put a smile on Virgo's face and make them laugh. If you do this while pulling back a little in order to give yourself poise and value, they will become very curious about you.

HOW TO KNOW IF VIRGOS LIKES YOU

Virgos will challenge you with their negative qualities to see if you will stick around. This is a big way to tell if they are fond of you. The very insecure

Virgos will need to know that you will love them at their worst and that you won't run away when things get tough. If Virgos respect you and wants to court you, they will often start to pick out your flaws as well, for they love in a way that strives to make those they are with the best version of themselves. If Virgos are tagging along with your friend group a lot, you can be sure that they want to be around you. Be sure to be quite consistent with Virgos, for if they misinterpret your feelings, they will turn cold and paranoid.

HOW VIRGOS ARE IN A RELATIONSHIP

Virgos need to feel needed in a relationship. They are very methodical and will take as long as they need to make sure that they are entering the right relationship. They bring this same methodical thinking to problem-solving and will always work to make things better in a relationship instead of simply giving up. Virgo will always be a dedicated spouse, and though predictable, they like to live on the wild side every once in a while.

VIRGOS' IDEAL DATE

Virgos love learning new things. Therefore, instead of taking them out for dinner, take them out to a cooking class so they can learn a new skill and do something methodical. They will love mixing things up, and they will be glad they left the security of their home to fill their mind with new knowledge.

HOW VIRGOS ARE IN THE BEDROOM

In the bedroom, Virgos need to be comfortable to blossom. They are very unselfish lovers and need to make sure that their partner is enjoying themselves before they can truly let loose. Touching Virgo's stomach while hooking up with them will drive them wild. Though peculiar, Virgos like to have conversations when they get down and dirty, because it helps them feel comfortable and takes their mind off of their thoughts (which are often racing).

HOW VIRGOS DEAL WITH HEARTBREAK

Virgos are not very trusting when it comes to lasting relationships, so they tend to anticipate broken hearts before they happen. They are analytical and observant and see things coming before they actually happen. During a heartbreak, they have already come up with a way to heal themselves and to distract from their hurt. In a way, Virgo started to mend from an impending heartbreak long before their heart is actually broken, speeding up the process.

HOW VIRGOS ARE AS FRIENDS

Virgos are gentle and kind friends. They tend to be shy, so they will not make the first move when meeting new people. They do not like to lead; they prefer to follow their friends and go with the flow. Their best friends adore their advice and problem-solving skills. Virgos tend to feel like they aren't doing enough in friendships, when in reality they give so much to their pals. Therefore, they need to find friends that are just as attentive to their needs, making Virgos feel accepted and less obligated to prove something. Virgos are usually at the center of lifelong friendships, for they value and get very close to those they harmonize with.

HOW TO GAIN VIRGOS' RESPECT

Virgos respect anyone who is very well put-together. They admire those who have something going for themselves and have a plan for their lives.

HOW VIRGOS ARE WHEN THEY'RE MAD

Virgos cannot express their feelings very easily, so they often bottle up their emotions until they blow up at very small things. They will slam doors and cry, scream, and throw temper tantrums. Virgos keep so much inside, and when they do boil over it can be awkward for the people they are around, for no one will know what to do about the uncharacteristic outburst.

HOW VIRGOS ARE WHEN THEY'RE SAD

When sad, Virgos tend to isolate themselves. They develop compulsions, cleaning and washing their hands obsessively to get out of their mind and mask their emotions through work.

SIMPLE THINGS THAT MAKE VIRGOS HAPPY

If you want to make Virgos the happiest person, make sure you take the time to let them know that you understand them. Nothing makes them feel more appreciated than that. Otherwise, Virgos are very practical at heart. They like gifts that are useful more than luxurious, but mixing a little luxury with the practical realm would bring joy to most Virgos. If your Virgo wants a new vacuum cleaner or really likes nice shaving cream, spring for the top of the line.

VIRGOS AT THEIR BEST

At their best, Virgos are skilled in so many areas. They have an eye for beauty that inspires a lot within them, and their protective nature is very nurturing for those who are lucky enough to experience it. Virgos will always strive to do the best possible job for others and care so deeply about being thoughtful and inclusive.

VIRGOS AT THEIR WORST

At times, Virgos can be hard to get to know. They are so scared of being rejected and misunderstood that they close themselves off and hide behind their shy nature. When they open up, however, they can be suffocating and overprotective. In smaller friend groups, Virgos can succumb to gossip.

WHAT VIRGOS FEAR THE MOST

Virgos hate chaos. They genuinely fear it. They like being on time and they like order. When things are not efficient and orderly, Virgos are terrified.

LIKELY OCCUPATIONS FOR VIRGOS

Known for their perfectionism, Virgos are very detail-oriented employees. They are very good with their memory, and they are great problem-solvers and abstract thinkers. They also tend to be very tidy and neat. Service jobs are the best for Virgos, because they go above and beyond and often do really well for themselves if tips are involved. Research, statistics, and other jobs that require meticulous thinking will actually be enjoyable for Virgos.

VIRGOS' LIKELY HEALTH CONCERNS

Virgos tend to be the most analytical sign in the zodiac, and that energy stays within the digestive tract. When Virgos worry, they can suffer from ulcers and other digestion problems. They must remember to relax, using things such as calming teas and soothing music to relieve stress and slow their minds.

WHERE TO TAKE VIRGOS ON VACATION

Virgos will always choose an educational trip over a trip where they simply lie down on a beach. They will want to visit a place that is rich in history like Germany or Paris, and they will absolutely adore getting taken around by tour guides while they learn everything they need to know about the cultures they are exploring.

VIRGOS' LEARNING STYLE

Virgos are very organizational and detail-oriented. They make amazing self-learners and can teach themselves just about anything. Online courses are where Virgos thrive.

VIRGOS' HUMOR

Virgos tend to use complaints to make people laugh. They will poke fun while being witty about the issues they have with the world, entertaining those around them easily.

VIRGOS' FAVORITE PASTIME

Virgos love to clean. If they express interest in spending the entire weekend reorganizing their record collection or dusting every fan in the house, don't try to talk them out of it. Cleaning is one of the ways Virgos process the world. They also really enjoy learning. If you are looking for ways to enjoy time together with Virgos, it helps if you also enjoy spending time taking in culture or learning new skills. Invite Virgos to see a documentary movie with you, or take a cooking class together.

WHAT TO SAY TO MOTIVATE YOUR VIRGO

In a world that keeps trying to cut corners, in a world that is quickening and moving at warp speed, you still stick up for detail, for perfection, and that is an amazing trait. You see things no one else sees, you are reliable, your words of advice motivate and inspire people, and you help everyone around you understand themselves a little more because you help to slow everything down. People admire you and appreciate your presence in their lives.

LIBRA

Ω

DATES	September 23 – October 23
SIGN	Scales
RULING PLANET	Venus
ZODIAC QUALITY	Cardinal
ELEMENT	Air
POSITIVE TRAITS	Charming, Attractive, Friendly
NEGATIVE TRAITS	Shallow, Fickle, Overly Sensitive

IF A LIBRA WAS...

A STARBUCKS DRINK:
Hot Chocolate

A COLOR:
Rose

A GREEK GOD:
Aphrodite—goddess of love, beauty, and desire

AN ADDICTION:
Sleeping Pills

AN ALCOHOLIC BEVERAGE:
Cosmopolitan

A DRUG:
Cannabis

IN A HIGH-SCHOOL CLIQUE:
The Popular Kids

A CITY:
Rio de Janeiro, Brazil

A HARRY POTTER HOUSE:
Hufflepuff

AN UNTRANSLATABLE FRENCH WORD:
Retrouvailles—reuniting with someone you haven't seen in a while

A KISS:
Fiery

A TEEN MOVIE:
John Tucker Must Die

A CLOTHING ITEM:
Oversized T-Shirt

A FAMOUS LANDMARK:
Mount Fuji

A SEASON:
Summer

LIBRA

PERSONALITY TRAITS

LIBRAS ARE KNOWN FOR THEIR OBSESSION with attractiveness and external orientation. They believe that looking good can bring them very far, and they have proven this on many occasions. However, Libras can also be called out for their vanity. They are serious, charming, graceful, and good humorists. They tend to be magnets for people, drawing many to them.

Libras are attractive; that has been deeply established in the zodiac. However, they also really admire harmony and are fond of being social. Though they often want things to go smoothly, Libras can stir up a lot of controversy with their attitude and behavior.

Libras cannot be rushed, and they demand space whenever they feel pressured or crowded. They are, however, not opposed to putting pressure on others and often think that it will add to their character.

Libras are magnetic, attractive, and highly sought-after individuals. However, Libras tend to be very outspoken, and their views can rub a lot of people the wrong way. They have to keep their interactions light to avoid any blunders.

LIBRA

COMPATIBILITY & RELATIONSHIPS

LIBRAS ARE EASYGOING, VERY LOVING, and a little lazy. They want a fairy tale and need a partner who will help cater to that fantasy. Because Aquarians are filled with passion, partnering with Libra would be an amazing match. Their vigor for life and social situations will create the perfect lifestyle for any Libra who loves to entertain and dream as well. At the same time, Libras can be a little unpredictable for some as they passionately support one cause today and completely change course the next. It's best to be flexible when loving Libras—don't expect them to rigidly adhere to every passion, hobby, cause, or obsession that seems to define them in any given moment. They are not easily defined.

LIBRA AND ARIES COMPATIBILITY: This is a relationship of two alphas, which can make it pretty challenging. The road may be bumpy, but when the emotional connection between these two is deep and enduring, challenges are minimized and they are a force to be reckoned with. They will be a power couple with a lively (and large) group of friends they adore. They should, however, allow each other plenty of space to do things independently because their interests may not always overlap.

LIBRA AND TAURUS COMPATIBILITY: There's a lot of potential for jealousy in this relationship, but it can work if Libra babies Taurus a bit and always makes it known that they are their number-one priority. Initially Taurus will think Libra is too flashy, but as soon as they are exposed to their softer side they will be won over. Similarly, Libras will love the sturdy foundation Taurus provides.

LIBRA AND GEMINI COMPATIBILITY: These two make great friends and exciting, happy lovers. They are naturally compatible and like to spend their time the same way (around people, having fun). They are a social couple that other couples aspire to be like.

LIBRA AND CANCER COMPATIBILITY: Cancer and Libra will get along well, and their biggest fight will be about whether to stay in or go out with friends. There are no big chemistry fireworks here, but that often simply means less drama and more harmony.

LIBRA AND LEO COMPATIBILITY: Leo and Libra both love the spotlight, but somehow they also aren't competitive with each other about it. They'd rather share it (rare for both signs) and let the light shine on how happy they make each other as a couple.

LIBRA AND VIRGO COMPATIBILITY: Virgo and Libra can be a stable couple that make each other perfectly happy. It might not all be vacations and fireworks, but they support each other and don't piss each other off. They both value harmony and don't like conflict for the sake of conflict. They'll be very good at communicating with each other and checking in to make sure they are both happy.

LIBRA AND LIBRA COMPATIBILITY: Libra are one sign that get along with their own sign very well. Since their values are so important to them, having someone with similar values is half the battle. Together they will have a very happy, balanced, healthy relationship where they support each other emotionally, are super loyal, and build each other up in social settings.

LIBRA AND SCORPIO COMPATIBILITY: This pair balances each other out well, because while Scorpio is emotional and very intense, Libra is very lighthearted and carefree. In social settings, each sign can handle their own at a party and don't rely on each other. While they both do well on their own, they are better together.

LIBRA AND SAGITTARIUS COMPATIBILITY: This is an outgoing couple with a lot of friends. They will try new things together, do a lot of activities, and generally be a positive presence in each other's lives, but the lack of mental and emotional connection will leave Libra feeling lonely.

LIBRA AND CAPRICORN COMPATIBILITY: Capricorn is a sign that can balance out a lot of signs like Gemini, Sag, Aries, and Leo, but they can also bring out the worst in other signs like Taurus and Libra who are a bit prone to materialism. The relationship will be perfectly harmonious and they won't fight; it's just that as partners, they don't make each other better people.

LIBRA AND AQUARIUS COMPATIBILITY: These two will have a super-strong mental connection. They'll love making friends at yoga class and hosting brunch complete with a post-brunch meditation. The relationship will feel light even as they have a serious connection, and they'll generally get along well.

LIBRA AND PISCES COMPATIBILITY: This pair is one of the strongest. Their loyalty to one another is what is so great. They each are really empathetic and would give anyone the shirt off their back. They make such a good team because when one is down the other steps up when they need to and vice versa. This relationship is a forever combination if you're lucky to find such a thing.

HOW TO ATTRACT LIBRAS

Libras love spontaneity. To attract them, you should show them how easy-going and versatile you are. If they see you go with the flow when plans change at the drop of a hat, they will be inspired by your personality. Libras know that people who are spontaneous and fun-loving will appeal to their need to be kept on their toes. If you really want to stir things up, don't ask to hang out with them at another time. Ask them to do something in a moment, and go with it. This will intrigue them beyond words.

HOW TO KNOW IF LIBRAS LIKE YOU

Libras are naturally charming and well-loved, which can be confusing when trying to figure out if they like you. Sometimes their friendliness can be misleading. Though it may be hard to muster the courage, if you want to know if a Libra likes you, ask around. If Libras have been asked if they are fond of someone, they will tell the truth. Their close friends will most definitely have the lowdown on their current crush.

HOW LIBRAS ARE IN A RELATIONSHIP

Libras want the perfect partner, so they may take a while before deciding to get into a relationship. Libras like to keep the peace, and they are happiest when their relationships are harmonized. It is very, very odd for Libras to be alone. They are not very independent, and it is unnatural for them to be without their partner. They enjoy connecting with others, and this does not change when in a partnership. As lovers, Libras are creative and expressive while still being balanced. They love satisfying their partner, and they are some of the strongest and most charming catches in the zodiac.

THE IDEAL DATE FOR LIBRAS

Libras love to be pampered and calm. Therefore, a lovely couples' massage would be an ideal date. Libra will feel the stress melting out of their life, and they will be able to enjoy how romantic the side-by-side massage truly is. Finish the night off by indulging in champagne and chocolate, and Libra will be in heaven.

HOW LIBRAS ARE IN THE BEDROOM

If you grab Libra's butt in the bedroom, they will heart you forever. Grab their lower back as well, and they may ask you to marry them. They enjoy being submissive in bed, but that doesn't mean they don't crave the act. Libras are actually heavily obsessed with sex, often associating it with falling in love.

HOW LIBRAS DEAL WITH HEARTBREAK

Libras are not as prideful as Leos, but they do have quite a large ego. Heartbreak leads to Libras experiencing insecurity, but they have such a natural charm to them that they will often find a replacement in no time. Since they cannot be alone, Libras move very quickly when rebounding to heal their broken pieces and pump up their ego again.

HOW LIBRAS ARE AS FRIENDS

Libras are excellent communicators and they have great taste, resulting in them being very, very popular. Libras can often be found with a posse of people around them. However, Libras don't let the popularity sway them, and they use their leadership role to be a mediator in their group of friends and are always there to give advice when their pals need it. Unfortunately, Libras find it difficult to keep a secret, and they may end up upsetting people they care about without intending to do so.

HOW TO GAIN A LIBRA'S RESPECT

Libras respect anyone who is witty. Libras also like confident people who have a lot going for them.

HOW LIBRAS ARE WHEN THEY'RE MAD

Libras absolutely hate conflict and confrontation. They despise it, and therefore it takes a lot for them to show their anger when they are mad. Since aggression is a very unpopular emotion, Libras have learned to keep it to themselves so as not to disturb their likeable, charming image. When they do fly off the handle, Libras often justify their meltdowns and believe that they expressed themselves in the best possible way.

HOW LIBRAS ARE WHEN THEY'RE SAD

When sad, Libras get quite moody. They are unstable and don't feel the need to socialize as much as they usually do. This causes them to feel a hopelessness within them, and they feel rejected and disliked by their posse.

When sad, Libras will always try to appear happy or pretend as if nothing is wrong. Their composure is seen as a survival tactic, for they fear if they break down or reveal any negative emotion, they will be seen differently in the public eye. Libras are silent sufferers.

SIMPLE THINGS THAT MAKE LIBRAS HAPPY

To be happy, Libras just want the freedom of choice. They love being able to do things, buy things, and obtain things without ever having to wait for them or ask for approval. They often prefer the finer things in life, meaning they are likely to spend more than more frugal signs to attain the objects they surround themselves with. But, the objects they choose tend to be special, precious, and well curated for sharing with others or becoming conversation pieces.

LIBRAS AT THEIR BEST

At their best, Libras are fun-loving people who think ahead. They are not to be underestimated, as they are seriously observant and have a lot to offer people who pick their brain. They are quirky and clever and have an artistic charm that is irresistible.

LIBRAS AT THEIR WORST

At their worst, Libras hide behind masks. You never know what they are truly feeling, and they put on an overly confident front to seem agreeable and charming. Behind the mask, Libra can be very self-doubting, lazy, and avoidant—the complete opposite of what they put out into the world.

WHAT LIBRAS FEAR THE MOST

Libras fear confrontation, and they will do absolutely everything in their power to keep things harmonious. They strive to make people happy. Libras are terrified of causing others distress and hurting the feelings of those around them. They never want to upset people, and it scares them to think they could potentially say or do something that would unintentionally stress someone out.

LIKELY OCCUPATIONS FOR LIBRAS

Libras are the full package when it comes to employees. They are charming, attractive, generous, and entertaining. They are cooperative, and they make amazing team leaders because of that. Libras would make fantastic customer-service employees because they are patient and fair. Working with people is their strong suit, so any job that caters to that would be a great fit for Libras. Jobs in politics, sales, negotiations, or travel would benefit from having Libras onboard.

LIBRAS' LIKELY HEALTH CONCERNS

Libras are ruled by their kidneys and their bladder. They are encouraged to drink a lot of clear water and to keep clarity in their relationships to promote balance in their body.

WHERE TO TAKE LIBRAS ON VACATION

Libras will pick a vacation based on their mood. It is a great idea for Libras to focus on places that offer access to other, aesthetically different destinations. For example, the Greek islands would stimulate Libras' many personalities and moods, with islands that are known for partying, islands that are known for extreme relaxation, and islands that are known for culinary experiences.

LIBRAS' LEARNING STYLE

Libras learn in social situations and independent situations. They need the balance and would excel in a classroom that was harmonized between online work and hands-on work. Study groups are great assets for Libras.

LIBRAS' HUMOR

Libras tend to be extremely sarcastic, and they love to tell stories that end in howling laughter. Libras are entertainers who will always go on a tangent and tell a long-winded memory for a laugh. There's no stopping them when they get started.

FAVORITE PASTIME FOR LIBRAS

Libras love spending time with the person they care for. They enjoy video games, research, and joking around.

WHAT TO SAY TO MOTIVATE YOUR LIBRA

Your personality is just stunning. Your ideas hold so much merit and thought that they can truly change the world if you simply put them to good use. Don't let people push you around. Don't allow for people who may not understand you to make you feel unworthy of success, love, and happiness. You are worth so much. Your heart is worth so much. Have pride in how unique you are. Take all of what you hold within you and run with it— spread it around, and you will see just how much you inspire.

SCORPIO

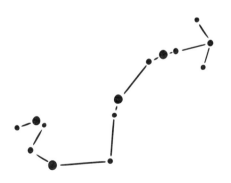

DATES	October 23 – November 22
SIGN	Scorpion
RULING PLANET	Mars
ZODIAC QUALITY	Fixed
ELEMENT	Water
POSITIVE TRAITS	Dominant, Controlled, Passionate
NEGATIVE TRAITS	Stubborn, Angry, Overly Emotional

IF SCORPIO WAS...

A STARBUCKS DRINK:
Iced Caramel Macchiato

A COLOR:
Scarlet Red

A GREEK GOD:
Ares—god of war

AN ADDICTION:
Internet Addiction

AN ALCOHOLIC BEVERAGE:
Tequila

A DRUG:
Heroin

IN A HIGH-SCHOOL CLIQUE:
Goth Kids

A CITY:
New York City

A HARRY POTTER HOUSE:
Ravenclaw

AN UNTRANSLATABLE FRENCH PHRASE:
Jolie laide—beautiful ugly

A KISS:
Intense

A TEEN MOVIE:
10 Things I Hate About You

A CLOTHING ITEM:
Little Black Dress

A FAMOUS LANDMARK:
The Pyramids

A SEASON:
Winter

SCORPIO

PERSONALITY TRAITS

SCORPIOS ARE KNOWN TO BE INTENSE CREATURES. Their presence holds a lot of weight and aggression. They are known to be figures of great power and control.

Scorpios have an incredible ability to deny themselves human contact. They methodically deal with serious situations. Known for their sexual prowess and energies, Scorpios are often very fond of mysteries and metamorphosis.

Scorpios are often dominant figures in their family, social, and work groups. They are known to emphasize their powerful, sexual, and dynamically deep aspects, but they can also be belligerent. When ignored, Scorpios react in a strong manner. They will never confront someone, but they will keep their guard up until they have a perfect moment to unleash their words and fury on someone. They always have something up their sleeve, and they hold grudges for insanely long periods.

Scorpios carry around a very strong understanding of life's seriousness. They are aware of the tragic nature of it all, and therefore they are suspicious creatures who dislike over-optimistic philosophies and superficial attitudes that sugarcoat the human condition. However, they are not all dark. They do have a sense of humor, and they understand that life is filled with irony. They have a lot of tendencies that lean toward self-destruction, so Scorpios need to be careful when it comes to controlling behavior, addiction, and attachment.

SCORPIO

COMPATIBILITY & RELATIONSHIPS

SCORPIOS ARE INTENSE, STUBBORN, AND FUNNY at the same time. They are confusing creatures. They need to find a partner that can handle their intense emotions and mood swings without getting sucked into their dark minds. Scorpios need someone who will love them through those periods of intensity and will know when to leave them alone and when to keep them close. Capricorn would be an amazing match for Scorpio, because they are patient enough to deal with Scorpios' many personalities.

SCORPIO AND ARIES COMPATIBILITY: This is a toxic combination. Each is a hothead. Each gets angry very quickly. And each is very competitive. They each strive to be the dominant ones in relationships and fight for power. They each come across as overly confident and a little too blunt sometimes, so the things that do come out of their mouths when fighting aren't nice.

SCORPIO AND TAURUS COMPATIBILITY: This is arguably the worst combination of any two signs. This pair seems to bring out the absolute worst in each other, like a tornado coming into each other's lives and ruining everything about the other person. There are some people who shouldn't be together, and this duo is toxic.

SCORPIO AND GEMINI COMPATIBILITY: This pair is almost too alike to function as healthy partners. They each can be stubborn and cold. They never think they are wrong and struggle in owning up to it when they are. Their fights are always very intense. While they each have an acid tongue, they tend to say things they later regret.

SCORPIO AND CANCER COMPATIBILITY: Many believe this is the best match in the entire zodiac. These two signs understand and complement each other perfectly, even though on the surface they seem to have different personalities. What works here is that each person in the relationship is strong where the other is weak. They're both very interested in having a strong relationship (something they're willing to put work into), and they have similar goals in life they want to work together to achieve.

SCORPIO AND LEO COMPATIBILITY: In a relationship, Leo needs to be in the spotlight and Scorpios let them have it. While Scorpios know when to fight their battles and choose them wisely, the biggest issue this pair has is a fight for power.

SCORPIO AND VIRGO COMPATIBILITY: This isn't the best combination there is. But it also isn't the worst. Together the strong parts of the relationship come out in the form of support. They each work hard and are motivated and driven. They each care a lot about being successful. The relationship isn't the number-one priority for either of them, but they respect that. While it's a healthy relationship, it's not the one that sends you head over heels.

SCORPIO AND LIBRA COMPATIBILITY: This pair balances each other out so well, because while Scorpios are emotional and intense, Libras are lighthearted and carefree. In social settings, each sign can handle their own at a party and don't rely on each other. While they both do well on their own, they are better together.

SCORPIO AND SCORPIO COMPATIBILITY: Almost more than any other sign in the zodiac, Scorpios need someone to complement them, not replicate them. There's a reason you never hear Scorpios say, "I married my best friend!" Another Scorpio will put Scorpio on the defensive, and they won't be able to feel comfortable enough to open up and enjoy any of a relationship's loving aspects.

SCORPIO AND SAGITTARIUS COMPATIBILITY: Each sign is very stubborn, but they never stop fighting for each other. Even though they have strong personalities, it seems to work because they make such a good team and really support each other. Problems occur between this pair when one becomes too stubborn to apologize.

SCORPIO AND CAPRICORN COMPATIBILITY: This is the relationship you're lucky to find when you're ready to settle down. Scorpios commit later in their lives after they have had fun and want something serious, while Capricorn was ready for that all along. Scorpio can be needy, but if you ask Capricorn, being understanding, observant, and giving Scorpio space when they need it is easy. Scorpios' personalities change frequently, and what makes Capricorn a good partner is that they strive to be what Scorpio needs all the time, getting fulfillment and happiness out of playing that role.

SCORPIO AND AQUARIUS COMPATIBILITY: While Scorpios might take things to heart and read people very closely, Aquarians have the ability to brush things off. They will give Scorpios the time they need to come back to them. They will never overwhelm them with attention, and they don't need much themselves besides the loyalty that comes with being with Scorpios.

SCORPIO AND PISCES COMPATIBILITY: Like the saying "opposites attract," no truer statement applies to this pair. Scorpios are cold and guarded. They struggle in trusting people and letting anyone in. They always want to be the dominant one in a relationship. Pisces, on the other hand, tends to be passive, wearing their heart on their sleeve and loving Scorpios as hard as they possibly can. And while it's a challenge once they have Scorpios' trust, what makes this bond so strong is the loyalty to one another.

HOW TO ATTRACT SCORPIO

Scorpio will make you prove your feelings for them. You will need to pay attention to them and learn them. Remembering things they say, recalling their motivations and their aspirations will show Scorpio whom you are trying to court that you are serious about them. If Scorpio tells you that they are fond of you, do not play any games. You have passed their test, and you must let them know that you reciprocate their feelings, or else they will feel rejected.

HOW TO KNOW IF SCORPIO LIKES YOU

If you are trying to figure out whether Scorpio likes you, pay attention to how they behave around you. Are they giving you extra attention in public? That is a telltale sign that they are fond of you, because Scorpios do not bother wasting their time with people who do not intrigue them. Around their crush, Scorpios can be really awkward, and you may not realize that they like you because of that. If Scorpio makes intense eye contact with you and stares at you often, this is another big sign. Scorpios are known to speak with their eyes, so if they are focused on you, you have them right where you want them.

HOW SCORPIOS ARE IN A RELATIONSHIP

Scorpios are incredibly passionate when in a relationship. They take intimacy and closeness seriously, because they do not trust many people. Scorpios think that intelligent and honest partners are wonderful, and they need to be with someone who can keep them interested and intrigued. Relationships will always take time with Scorpio, but once devoted to someone, they are the most loyal sign in the zodiac. Scorpios are so loyal, they often stay with people long after the spark is gone, which is one of their biggest downfalls.

IDEAL DATE FOR SCORPIO

All Scorpio needs on a date is alone time. Therefore, a night in with just the two of you will be the best possible scenario for reclusive Scorpio. Make sure to create a little oasis for you and your partner. Things such as candles, good music, food, and wine will appeal to Scorpio's sensual side, and it will create a hedonistic environment that they will enjoy distraction-free.

HOW SCORPIOS ARE IN THE BEDROOM

Everyone knows that Scorpios are the biggest freaks in the zodiac. They love oral sex and are very dominant in bed. They enjoy a partner whom they can get cheeky with and are usually very intense underneath the sheets. They require an active and adventurous partner in the bedroom.

HOW SCORPIOS DEAL WITH HEARTBREAK

Scorpios may never talk about their feelings, but they are extremely emotional. They are considered to be some of the deepest people in the zodiac. Therefore, when Scorpios are dealing with heartbreak, they feel their broken heart in full force. They feel hurt, sad, angry, betrayed, insecure, and confused all at the same time. These feelings will last a while before Scorpios slowly start to harmonize their life again.

HOW SCORPIOS ARE AS FRIENDS

Scorpios, although guarded at first, are some of the most loyal friends in the zodiac. They love being alone and having time to themselves, but they also enjoy having people around them when that aspect of their personality is turned on. They love surrounding themselves with likeminded people who understand them and can handle their depth. Scorpios want friends that are just as loyal as they are, and they need to know that they can trust those friends. Trust to Scorpios is absolutely everything; it is the cornerstone of every relationship and friendship they enter.

HOW TO GAIN A SCORPIO'S RESPECT

Scorpio will respect you if you show them that you are classy and a little weird. They like people who can relate to them when it comes to being odd and often admire those who are different than most people.

HOW SCORPIOS ARE WHEN THEY'RE MAD

It is rare to see an angry Scorpio, as they are so good at keeping their feelings locked away. However, when they are angry and you are in their line of fire, watch out. They will stare you down, and that eye contact will feel like cold knives. They can be very, very hurtful with their words, and their sarcasm can cause a lot of harm to those who have to deal with it. Scorpios also don't forget those who scorn them, and they will often hold grudges. They are emotionally destructive creatures.

HOW SCORPIOS ARE WHEN THEY'RE SAD

When sad, Scorpios like to isolate themselves. They can grow hostile and have violent mood swings. Their intensity causes extreme emotions within them, and this can manifest into paranoia. Scorpios may feel that it is them against the world and can become completely weighed down by that concept.

SIMPLE THINGS THAT MAKE SCORPIO HAPPY

Scorpio just wants to be understood and included. They are happiest when they are in a loving relationship.

SCORPIOS AT THEIR BEST

At their best, Scorpios are confident and determined individuals who are full of surprises. They are clever, and they always have something brewing in their minds. Their vision is incredible. Scorpios also foster a lot of willpower and are very dedicated and loyal to the things and the people they care about. They will always fight their own battles, and they never give up. They are dynamic, deep, and are so beautifully emotional when they are harmonized.

SCORPIOS AT THEIR WORST

At their worst, Scorpios tend to ramble and have a stubborn way of thinking that makes them believe in their wants above anything else. They can be overly confident when they are allowed to run with their ideas, and this can get them into a lot of trouble. They can offend a lot of people with their tendency to isolate themselves and shut down, and their need to be sneaky and controlling can cause those around them to feel manipulated and untrusting toward them.

WHAT SCORPIOS FEAR THE MOST

Scorpios fear failure and disappointing those they care most about. They are wildly insecure inside when it comes to certain things, and they fear that they will not live up to the expectations they set out for themselves and the dreams they foster. Above all else, Scorpios fear vulnerability, and they are afraid of others knowing their deepest feelings.

SCORPIO'S LIKELY OCCUPATIONS

Scorpios are intense and meticulous. They have an amazing capacity to block out distractions, concentrate, and focus on a task at hand. This would make them amazing surgeons. They are curious and intrigued by knowledge, which makes them amazing investigators and interrogators. Scorpios are independent, however, so they need a job with a lot of freedom and room to roam. They would make amazing detectives and kickass lawyers.

SCORPIO'S LIKELY HEALTH CONCERNS

Scorpios are ruled by the reproductive and excretory systems. Scorpios need to expel their emotions and they cannot repress their intensity, because it will cause them to become blocked and uncomfortable. They are easily thrown off when they allow deep thoughts or heavy emotions to fester, and they need to learn how to safely release mental and emotional burdens to find a truly healthy balance.

WHERE TO TAKE SCORPIO ON VACATION

Scorpios love to travel, but they don't ever want to go completely off the grid—they enjoy their luxurious comforts. Therefore, a beautiful island that houses stunning resorts would blow Scorpio's mind and appeal to their need for pampering while giving them a taste of the exotic.

SCORPIO'S LEARNING STYLE

Scorpios are investigators, so they are better suited to learn alone. They are also overachievers, often digging deeper than they should and learning more than they need to.

SCORPIO'S HUMOR

Scorpios are the rulers of sarcasm. They will always have something to say and can often come off as rude to those who do not know them well enough. They constantly comment on things and can use passive-aggressive humor to get their point across.

SCORPIO'S FAVORITE PASTIME

Scorpios love music, and they always enjoy watching movies—alone or with their significant other.

WHAT TO SAY TO MOTIVATE YOUR SCORPIO

You need to understand that good people exist in this world—you included. Please trust that not everyone is out to break your heart and hurt you. Not everyone has a hidden agenda. Your passion makes you feel the most incredible things, and when you push people away, you deny them the ability to experience how deep and beautiful you are inside. People need to experience that, because you hold within you a love that changes lives. Your loyalty, your depth—it is otherworldly. Being on the positive side of that will truly open up the world for you.

SAGITTARIUS

DATES	November 22 – December 21
SIGN	Archer
RULING PLANET	Jupiter
ZODIAC QUALITY	Mutable
ELEMENT	Fire
POSITIVE TRAITS	Funny, Adventurous, Curious
NEGATIVE TRAITS	Shallow, Flighty, Immature

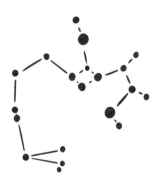

IF SAGITTARIUS WAS...

A STARBUCKS DRINK:
Skinny Vanilla Latte

A COLOR:
Magenta

A GREEK GOD:
Hestia—goddess of the hearth

AN ADDICTION:
Gambling

AN ALCOHOLIC BEVERAGE:
Sake

A DRUG:
PCP

IN A HIGH-SCHOOL CLIQUE:
Gamer Kids

A CITY:
Honolulu, Hawaii

A HARRY POTTER HOUSE:
Slytherin

AN UNTRANSLATABLE FRENCH WORD:
Spleen—boredom and dissatisfaction

A KISS:
Addictive

A TEEN MOVIE:
Easy A

A CLOTHING ITEM:
No clothes for a Sag. They love being naked/barefoot.

A FAMOUS LANDMARK:
Statue of Liberty

A SEASON:
Fall

SAGITTARIUS

PERSONALITY TRAITS

SAGITTARIANS SYMBOLIZE A GROWING human spirit. They represent liberation, optimism, and the refusal to sell themselves short to details and the status quo. They always see the bigger picture.

Sagittarius will often use their philosophy to solve problems in social situations. They want to help and get straight to the heart of the matter when they see issues arise. They tend to encourage people to see the best side of things and are very optimistic.

For Sagittarius, honesty of intention and belief are strong principles which they apply to themselves as well as to others. But although they generally have a peachy outlook on life, they usually get caught up in disputes due to their idealism.

Sagittarius will often be a forever student, exploring the world and trying to figure it out one spontaneous trip after the other. They crave knowledge and often find it tucked away in hard-to-reach places.

Sagittarius is revered in the zodiac for moving around so much. They cannot stay in one place, nor can they sit still. Rarely bored, these people often seek new ways to express themselves and their overactive mind.

SAGITTARIUS

COMPATIBILITY & RELATIONSHIPS

SAGITTARIUS PARTNERS ARE VERY INDEPENDENT and honest. They need someone in their life who will be able to come and go with them. Sagittarius needs a partner that will know when to stay back and when their love needs a partner in crime. Aries will always be up for wandering, and they are fiercely independent, so they will never feel left out when Sagittarius needs to explore. Aries/Sagittarius relationship are also filled with optimism, which will allow them to stand the test of time.

SAGITTARIUS AND ARIES COMPATIBILITY: These signs make a fun-loving couple who are always making each other laugh. They have a ton of inside jokes and prefer to keep things in their lives light and happy. They have a big circle of friends and are always planning fun things for everyone to do.

SAGITTARIUS AND TAURUS COMPATIBILITY: These signs make great friends, as they can appreciate fun and indulgence together, but they don't often make great couples. People born under Taurus tend to want to settle down, while Sagittarians tend to want to drift around. They aren't naturally suited to complement each other.

SAGITTARIUS AND GEMINI COMPATIBILITY: This pair falls very hard for each other. It's the love they each remember in their lives. While it starts off as a healthy relationship, Sagittarius begins to emotionally rely too heavily on Gemini so that Gemini ends up resenting them and calling it off.

They walk away still with a lot of respect, but for Sagittarius it's the hardest heartbreak they will get over in their life.

SAGITTARIUS AND CANCER COMPATIBILITY: It's hard to see why these two signs would get together, as they don't have similar values or personalities, but they also are both laid-back and like to avoid conflict, so they don't fight a lot as a couple. With the right two people, this could be an easy relationship celebrating the lighter side of Cancer and the deeper side of Sag.

SAGITTARIUS AND LEO COMPATIBILITY: This is a fun-loving couple that gets along well and typically has zero drama. They understand and appreciate each other's nature and would rather spend time doing than talking. They tend to be a busy couple who don't spend a lot of time at home.

SAGITTARIUS AND VIRGO COMPATIBILITY: This can be a good opposites-attract relationship, as the strengths and weaknesses of the two are complementary, and they aren't so opposite that they will drive each other crazy. Sagittarius will force Virgo to have fun, and Virgo will make sure Sagittarius doesn't fall off a cliff somewhere.

SAGITTARIUS AND LIBRA COMPATIBILITY: This is an outgoing couple with a lot of friends. They will try new things together, do a lot of activities, and generally be a positive presence in each other's lives, but the lack of mental and emotional connection will leave Libra feeling a bit lonely.

SAGITTARIUS AND SCORPIO COMPATIBILITY: Each sign is very stubborn, but they never stop fighting for each other. Even though they have strong personalities, it seems to work with each other because they make such a good team and really do support each other. Problems occur between this pair when one becomes too stubborn to apologize.

SAGITTARIUS AND SAGITTARIUS COMPATIBILITY: Sagittarius gets along with their own sign really well. There won't be anyone there to mother them—which can get them into trouble—but they don't value having things work out perfectly anyway, so it's not a big loss. They'll have a lot of fun, not fight, and be a laid-back couple that always does exactly what they want to do.

SAGITTARIUS AND CAPRICORN COMPATIBILITY: These signs are not alike in what they value or in personality type. They truly do not like fundamental things about who the other person is or what they want and will quickly grow resentful of each other and bicker a lot.

SAGITTARIUS AND AQUARIUS COMPATIBILITY: This is a good match, as both signs are curious explorers. They won't hold each other back, and they'll be happy partners exploring ideas and the world together.

SAGITTARIUS AND PISCES COMPATIBILITY: Emotionally, this combination balances each other out very well. They each are hopeless romantics and wear their heart on their sleeve, and they respect that about each other. They are empathetic and understanding and truly vibe with what each is feeling and trying to be what each person needs in the relationship. The only problem that occurs in this type of relationship is that because the level of intense emotions between the two is sometimes too dramatic, they need someone a little bit different.

HOW TO ATTRACT SAGITTARIUS

To attract Sagittarius, all you have to do is share your passions with them. Talk to them about your dreams and all of the things you want to achieve. Tell them about your hobbies, your wildest thoughts, your fantasies, and all of your achievements. They will feed off of your ambition, and they will want to be part of the life you are creating for yourself. If you can meet them with the same enthusiasm for their own dreams and goals, they will not be able to resist you.

HOW TO KNOW IF SAGITTARIUS LIKES YOU

If Sagittarius likes you, you can expect that they will try to make you laugh. They will go out of their way to make you smile. They will be playful with you, and they will try to impress you with all of their funny skills and odd behaviors. If Sagittarius really likes you, they will stutter and act shy around you—something that rarely happens with Sagittarius. Expect to be complimented a lot when Sagittarius is courting you.

HOW SAGITTARIUS IS IN A RELATIONSHIP

In a relationship, Sagittarius is often very energetic and inquisitive. They are the adventurers of the zodiac, and they have a very open-minded approach to life and partnerships. They will want to wander—it is within them to do so—and they will always search for the meaning of life in their travels, so traveling is extremely important to them. It will be very difficult to get Sagittarius to settle down, and they often favor open relationships. They adore change, and they crave it in order to feel good about themselves, so being tied down is something that will only cause them to feel burdened and trapped.

SAGITTARIUS'S IDEAL DATE

If you want to bring Sagittarius on a kickass date, bring them on a hike. Outdoorsy Sagittarius will enjoy being in nature, as they always get overwhelmed when inside. Catering to their need to explore and find adventure, taking them outside of stuffy restaurants and apartments is key, and they will appreciate your thirst for wandering.

HOW SAGITTARIUS IS IN THE BEDROOM

Sagittarius lovers adore sex in odd places. They are adventurers, and adding a little bit of spontaneity to their physical antics energizes them. They will initiate sex whenever they get the urge, and they will pay no mind to where they are. They are kinky and will try harder in bed when they really like you.

HOW SAGITTARIUS DEALS WITH HEARTBREAK

Sagittarius is a truly independent sign in the zodiac. Though they do care about being heartbroken, they truly will not dwell on it, and they will never let it hold them back. Due to their fleeting tendencies in relationships, Sagittarians will move on quickly and find a new, exciting, adventurous conquest to ease them into a new chapter.

HOW SAGITTARIANS ARE AS FRIENDS

If you have Sagittarius as a friend, you are guaranteed to have a lot of fun. They are adventurers and explorers, and they are in love with freedom and liberation. They will always be up for exciting things and are the kind of friend you want by your side when you travel and find new places to dig your feet into. Sagittarius pals are adored for bringing the unexpected to other people's lives. Friends that are easygoing and not needy are embraced by the wide-eyed Sag.

HOW TO GAIN SAGITTARIUS'S RESPECT

To impress Sagittarius, stimulate them. They appreciate and respect people with goals and will always admire those who have explored the world.

HOW SAGITTARIANS ARE WHEN THEY'RE MAD

When mad, Sagittarians get angry flare-ups and use hurtful words to really burn people. If you upset Sagittarius, they will unfriend you from all social media immediately. They will also do so in real life, often ignoring people who have slighted them and pretending they don't even know them at all.

HOW SAGITTARIANS ARE WHEN THEY'RE SAD

When sad, Sagittarius gets emotionally exhausted. This lethargy turns physical when the sadness increases, and they often resort to substance abuse to feel alive. They are escapists and will run away at the drop of a hat to feed their soul and shock it back into feeling happy again.

SIMPLE THINGS THAT MAKE SAGITTARIUS HAPPY

Sagittarius loves having fun friends around them and will always say yes to an adventure. Exploring makes them truly happy. One of the best things you can give Sagittarius is the space and freedom to venture out into nature or travel to recharge their batteries.

SAGITTARIANS AT THEIR BEST

At their best, Sagittarians are extremely loyal, strong, and faithful to their beliefs. They have a variety of interests, and they are extremely diverse human beings. They will always make something work because they will never give up when things get tough. They are experts at moving on, and they can rebuild themselves time and time again whenever things turn sour due to their incredible strength and independence.

SAGITTARIUS AT THEIR WORST

At their worst, Sagittarians simply hear what they want to hear, and this can often cause them to disregard others and the feelings they hold. Sagittarians often interrupt people, and they don't allow others to get many words in, which makes people feel inferior and upset. They can take things too far, and they never pick up on the fact that they have hurt others—they are oblivious.

WHAT SAGITTARIUS FEARS THE MOST

Due to their never-ending energy, Sagittarius often fears being controlled by others. They desire to explore and live their lives as freely as possible. They are terrified of settling for a life that is not filled with all of the things they associate with personal freedom, and they cannot stand the idea of being trapped in mediocrity.

SAGITTARIUS'S LIKELY OCCUPATIONS

Ethical, full of energy, and extremely insightful, Sagittarians are amazing decision-makers and make very easygoing bosses. Due to their spiritual tendencies and their connection to nature, Sagittarians are often well-equipped for a career that deals with the environment or animals. A job that puts them outside or one that allows for them to travel the world is a big bonus for Sagittarius. They would make amazing coaches and tour guides, because they would not be tied down by those careers—they could do them anywhere in the world, manifesting their need for freedom and flightiness.

SAGITTARIUS'S LIKELY HEALTH CONCERNS

Sagittarius is ruled by the thighs and the sciatic nerve. The best way to keep themselves healthy would be to exercise often while focusing primarily on the legs and back. Leg cramps and back pain can often occur when Sagittarius is bogged down in normal life, so they must get out into nature to unwind and relax.

WHERE TO TAKE SAGITTARIUS ON VACATION

Sagittarius is known to be one of the most adventurous signs in the zodiac. They will completely immerse themselves in the culture of another country. They will blend in with locals, learn new languages, and so on. They often choose Airbnbs and camping over hotels, and they need a place that offers them a lot of stimulation. A place like South Africa would be an amazing fit for Sagittarius, because it offers a one-of-a-kind outdoor experience.

SAGITTARIUS LEARNING STYLE

Sagittarius is the philosopher and adventurer of the zodiac, so they need a lot of hands-on learning experiences. Field trips and cultural exchange programs are amazing options for Sagittarius who wants to increase their knowledge. However, Sagittarius is not a fan of overly structured or rigid learning experiences. It's best for them to have some freedom to explore.

SAGITTARIUS HUMOR

Sagittarius will turn everything into a funny joke or a hilarious story. They have observational and sarcastic moments when it comes to humor, and those harmonize well to make these easygoing Sags the life of the party when they get rolling.

FAVORITE PASTIME FOR SAGITTARIUS

Sagittarius loves hiking, listening to music, and they adore hanging out with friends on an adventure. If they could travel or spend much of their time outdoors, it's likely they would.

WHAT TO SAY TO MOTIVATE YOUR SAGITTARIUS

Please understand that you do not have to destroy yourself to feel better. You are so fun to be around and you hold adventure within you unlike any other. People want to be around you because you have a way of captivating them. Don't get addicted to that, though. You have the ability to be alone, and you are strong enough to stand on your own. You are strong enough to go on your own adventures, to make your life your own. Go out and live for yourself.

CAPRICORN

♑

DATES	December 21 – January 20
SIGN	Fish/Goat Hybrid
RULING PLANET	Saturn
ZODIAC QUALITY	Cardinal
ELEMENT	Earth
POSITIVE TRAITS	Ambitious, Protective, Stylish
NEGATIVE TRAITS	Superficial, Dishonest, Boring

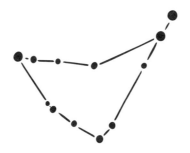

IF A CAPRICORN WERE...

A STARBUCKS DRINK:
Vanilla Bean Frap

A COLOR:
Navy Blue

A GREEK GOD:
Hermes—god of boundaries

AN ADDICTION:
Working

AN ALCOHOLIC BEVERAGE:
Dry Martini

A DRUG:
Ritalin

IN A HIGH-SCHOOL CLIQUE:
AP Scholars

A CITY:
Montreal, Canada

A HARRY POTTER HOUSE:
Ravenclaw

AN UNTRANSLATABLE FRENCH WORD:
Dépaysement—disorientation one feels when in a completely foreign setting

A KISS:
Lingering

A TEEN MOVIE:
The Breakfast Club

A CLOTHING ITEM:
Sneakers

A FAMOUS LANDMARK:
Great Wall of China

A SEASON:
Winter

CAPRICORN

PERSONALITY TRAITS

CAPRICORNS ARE SERIOUSLY MATURE and aware of how individualistic they are. They are associated with a careful approach and a very responsible attitude.

Perseverance, heart, and a drive to succeed are all symbolized by these ambitious people. Fortunately, their ability to reach the top and find success in all of their endeavors is a very large aspect of their personality as well.

Capricorns add a very mature, structural support to the zodiac. They can be hardened in their thoughts and ideas and are often extremely headstrong. Capricorns often limit, rather than expand, and that is due to their conservative nature. They believe that they can achieve everything they dream of if they just stay focused and keep their eye on the prize. They are patient and persistent, and they do not care how long it takes them to achieve what they have set out to achieve.

Capricorns are extremely difficult to pin down and characterize, because they embody so many varying personality types. However, mostly every Capricorn has accepted the fact that trials, difficulty, and suffering are a large part of life. They are very suspicious when things are too easy, and they hate when things are going too well. They can never sit still in those situations, because they are simply waiting for something to go wrong.

Capricorns know how power works, and they are very knowledgeable in their capacity to manifest it. They need to be careful, however, because they could end up becoming dictators rather than great leaders.

CAPRICORN

COMPATIBILITY & RELATIONSHIPS

CAPRICORNS ARE RESERVED, CAUTIOUS, and responsible. They are not always easy to win over and are best suited for a partner that will give them all of the tender love they want. However, they need to also let Capricorn's responsibility flourish without reprimanding them for being too serious. A Cappy wants to be appreciated for who they are; they cannot help the fact that they are steady beings. Tauruses are a perfect match for Capricorn, because both signs choose security over flightiness and appreciate familiarity and comfort.

CAPRICORN AND ARIES COMPATIBILITY: There's not a lot that Aries and Capricorn have in common, and both types aren't the kind of person to slow their roll for someone else. Capricorns are more conservative and wants to protect what they put out into the world more than Aries's look-before-you-leap nature allows them. Aries's least favorite thing in the world is feeling like someone is holding them back, so they'll struggle with Capricorn trying to control them.

CAPRICORN AND TAURUS COMPATIBILITY: Taurus and Capricorn are natural allies. They both love to indulge in the finer things in life, are ambitious, and like to show off a little bit. They fit together well and can be a very happy power couple.

CAPRICORN AND GEMINI: This couple can make it work even though they aren't naturally compatible. Gemini can draw Capricorn out of their conservative shell, and Capricorn can provide the structure Gemini needs to truly thrive. As long as they are patient with each other and their differences, they can make a great couple.

CAPRICORN AND CANCER COMPATIBILITY: It will be a bit of a struggle for these two to align their values, but they're not totally incompatible. Capricorn will seem a bit shallow to Cancer until they explain that they like nice things because it creates a relaxing home environment (among other things). That's a goal they are happy to work toward together, and Capricorn will appreciate how loyal Cancer is. Both will prize the relationship above all else.

CAPRICORN AND LEO COMPATIBILITY: An unlikely pairing, but one that can create a strong couple. Leo and Capricorn both appreciate being respected and appreciated by their peers and will work together to guard their privacy and make sure their reputations are what they desire. Neither is too wild, and while Capricorns can be prudish, that generally ends behind closed doors, which is all that matters to Leo.

CAPRICORN AND VIRGO COMPATIBILITY: This is a power couple in the making. Both people are ambitious, hardworking, and somewhat conservative when it comes to their personal lives. They will take a while to open up and be vulnerable with each other, but their interests are so aligned that once that happens, they'll be a perfect team.

CAPRICORN AND LIBRA COMPATIBILITY: Capricorn is a sign that can balance out a lot of signs like Gemini, Sag, Aries, and Leo, but they can also bring out the worst in other signs like Taurus and Libra, who are a bit prone to materialism. The relationship will be perfectly harmonious and they won't fight; it's just that as a partner they don't make each other better people.

CAPRICORN AND SCORPIO COMPATIBILITY: This is the relationship you're lucky to find when you're ready to settle down. Scorpio commits later in their life after they have had fun and want something serious, and Capricorn was simply ready for that all along. Scorpio's needs are a lot sometimes, but if you ask Capricorn, being understanding, observant, and giving Scorpio space when they need it is easy.

CAPRICORN AND SAGITTARIUS COMPATIBILITY: These signs are not alike in what they value or in personality type. They truly do not like fundamental things about who the other person is or what they want and will quickly grow resentful of each other and bicker a lot.

CAPRICORN AND CAPRICORN COMPATIBILITY: This is an ideal match, as Capricorn's values are so important to them that having someone with a duplicate set of ideals is their dream. They will understand each other's wants and needs so well and work as a team toward their shared goals. They will have unquestioned loyalty and guard their relationship above all else.

CAPRICORN AND AQUARIUS COMPATIBILITY: This is a hard relationship to get going, as they don't live similar lifestyles. The one thing that could make it work is Capricorn and Aquarius's shared interests in classical ideas—philosophy and art. If they can build a solid foundation of friendship based on common interests, they might begin to understand and meet each other's needs.

CAPRICORN AND PISCES COMPATIBILITY: This pair is one that probably started off as friends first, with each wondering who was going to make the first move and when. Any relationship that starts as a friendship you know will be one that's loyal and long-lasting. It's the relationship that comes into one another's lives when everyone is tired of getting hurt and played. It's the relationship that makes them feel safe and secure.

HOW TO ATTRACT CAPRICORN

Capricorns feel most comfortable around people who are like them, so if you are trying to attract one, be sure to mirror them. Reflect their body language, their attitude, their emotion, and they will feel like you are one of them. If you dress like them and talk like them, they will notice you even more and will be deeply attracted to you. However, you need to do this genuinely, for if Capricorn feels like you are laying it on too thick, they will feel as if they cannot trust you and will not be able to relate to you.

HOW TO KNOW IF CAPRICORN LIKES YOU

If Capricorn likes you, they will be very hot and cold. One day they will be flirting with you, and the next day they will avoid you. This is due to their overthinking; they don't want to seem too eager and will often choose indifference after a day of affection. Capricorns need to feel superior, and having a crush makes them feel weak. This often causes them to break things off before they even start, because they do not want to risk being hurt. However, if you make them feel secure and show Capricorn that you, too, think they are wonderful, they will stick around and eventually admit their feelings for you. Pay attention to the advice you get from Capricorn; it is a very big sign of affection. Capricorns want to make sure you know about all of their unique talents, and this is their way of impressing you. They will make eye contact with you if they are fond of you and will often stare at you intensely if they develop feelings for you.

HOW CAPRICORNS ARE IN A RELATIONSHIP

In a relationship, Capricorn will take things very slowly. Sometimes they will be painfully slow when entering a partnership, because it takes a long time for them to feel secure in their decisions. They will always take things one step at a time. Their words are sparse, but in a relationship Capricorn loves through action, so pay attention to how they act around you. You can usually figure out what is going through their mind by assessing their body language and their effort. Capricorns are genuine, generous, and sincere, and if they tell you that they love you, know that those words hold a lot of meaning to them.

IDEAL DATE FOR CAPRICORN

Capricorns are foodies, and they love trying new places where most people have not been. Figure out what the newest openings are in town and work your magic to get a reservation at the hottest new dining spot. Your Capricorn will appreciate the exclusivity, and they will love that they can be among the first few to talk about the experience. You'll hit it out of the park and appeal to Capricorn's admiration for the superior things in life.

HOW CAPRICORNS ARE IN THE BEDROOM

Capricorns are very serious when it comes to sex. They obsess about it, and they also avoid it. It depends on how they are feeling at that moment. They will either want lovely sex or rough sex. They will either want a casual hook-up or a steamy session with someone they are close to. They are all over the place, but they always know what they want when an opportunity presents itself, and they will turn it down if it doesn't match their mood.

HOW CAPRICORNS DEAL WITH HEARTBREAK

Capricorns will usually accept a broken heart. They are hell-bent on proving themselves, so a broken heart is just another opportunity to do better and to excel in difficult situations. This is also how Capricorns distract themselves from hurtful feelings.

HOW CAPRICORNS ARE AS FRIENDS

As friends, Capricorns are very interested in filling their free time with people who hold superior jobs in society. They want friends in high places. They will always try to go to the most selective and popular places in town to rub shoulders with those they want to befriend. When they do make a friend that they trust and isn't too needy, they often keep them for life, as they are rare and Capricorns admire that.

HOW TO GAIN THE RESPECT OF CAPRICORN

To gain Capricorn's respect, you must be confident. They are impressed by those who appeal to the inner snob they hold within them, so if you hold a high place in society you can guarantee that Cappy will find you admirable.

HOW CAPRICORNS ARE WHEN THEY'RE MAD

Though Capricorns are very easily angered, they will never show it. It is only when they are pushed to their limits that they will finally express their aggression. They will smash things, and they will criticize until their opponent is left with emotional wounds. Capricorns are the type of people who will say something like, "I'm not mad, I'm disappointed" to cut someone deeper than they need to. They strive to make people feel terrible about themselves when they are mad.

HOW CAPRICORNS ARE WHEN THEY'RE SAD

When sad, Capricorn succumbs to their overthinking. They lose all of their motivation to push themselves, and they often get extremely tired—both emotionally and physically. They will grow tense, and life will not impress them until they start to feel better.

SIMPLE THINGS THAT MAKE CAPRICORN HAPPY

Capricorns are happiest when they are rewarded for being good at something. They love getting praise.

CAPRICORNS AT THEIR BEST

At their best, Capricorns are a very relaxed people. They are always open to listen to people when they need them, and they will check up on friends they are worried about. They take things as they come, are very faithful and loyal, and they try their hardest to foster a lot of optimism in their life.

CAPRICORNS AT THEIR WORST

At their worst, Capricorns are always hiding some aspect of themselves from their friends, because they are so serious about being composed. They use silence as a weapon and are master manipulators. When angered they can be extremely mean, and they go to extremes when their emotions are not balanced.

WHAT CAPRICORNS FEAR THE MOST

Capricorn's main goal is to achieve everything they have ever dreamed of. They are full of ambition and motivation, and their drive is inspirational. Underneath it all, however, they are extremely scared that they are not good enough or talented enough to meet their expectations. They often fear that no one understands what they are trying to do with their life.

CAPRICORN'S LIKELY OCCUPATIONS

Capricorns love to be challenged, and they are always ambitious and up for a lot of work. They are determined, persistent, and they will do whatever it takes to meet their potential. Responsible, serious, and very aware of their surroundings, they are the most power-hungry sign in the zodiac. They enforce rules very well, and they keep schedules tight. They would make brilliant managers and bankers, and they would excel in science-based research projects.

CAPRICORN'S LIKELY HEALTH CONCERNS

Capricorns are ruled by their skeletal structure. If Capricorns become too rigid in their thinking or their lifestyle, they are likely to suffer from arthritis, rheumatism, and fragile bones. They need to focus on eating healthy and always incorporating sources of calcium into their diets.

WHERE TO TAKE CAPRICORN ON VACATION

Capricorns don't like to travel alone, and they often like utilizing their vacations as opportunities to reconnect with friends. Though they like to kick back and relax, Cappy needs stimulation in small doses in case they start to get bored of sitting around. A boat cruise would be an amazing vacation for Capricorn, because they can soak up the sun during the day and explore different cities and harbors when the boat anchors.

CAPRICORN'S LEARNING STYLE

Capricorns are traditionalists. They take things slowly and learn in steps. They will excel in a good old-fashioned classroom, and they will often overachieve in programs that help them progress faster than their peers.

CAPRICORN'S HUMOR

Capricorns are the bluffing pros in the zodiac. They can keep a straight face and then they will suddenly burst out laughing at themselves. People can't help but laugh with them when this happens.

CAPRICORN'S FAVORITE PASTIME

Capricorns love learning and organizing. They also enjoy listening to music and relaxing with their most trusted friends.

WHAT TO SAY TO MOTIVATE YOUR CAPRICORN

You don't always have to be the person who is solely focused on money and success. You have to understand that those things do not define you. You are worth so much more. You can be yourself. You can live without worrying about your next step and the step after that. You can relax. You don't have to push people away; they are not going to ruin your progress or hurt you. Open yourself up to love and simplicity. You need the balance, and you flourish when it graces your life.

AQUARIUS

DATES	January 20 – February 18
SIGN	Water-bearer
RULING PLANET	Saturn
ZODIAC QUALITY	Fixed
ELEMENT	Air
POSITIVE TRAITS	Dreamy, Independent, Intelligent
NEGATIVE TRAITS	Erratic, Impractical, Unemotional

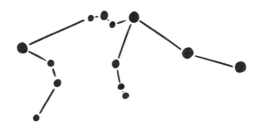

IF AQUARIUS WAS...

A STARBUCKS DRINK:
Peppermint Mocha

A COLOR:
Electric Blue

A GREEK GOD:
Poseidon—god of the sea

AN ADDICTION:
Video Games

AN ALCOHOLIC BEVERAGE:
Jägermeister

A DRUG:
Mushrooms

IN A HIGH-SCHOOL CLIQUE:
Band Geeks

A CITY:
Dubai, UAE

A HARRY POTTER HOUSE:
Ravenclaw

AN UNTRANSLATABLE FRENCH PHRASE:
A l'ouest—describing someone a little strange or different

A KISS:
Sloppy

A TEEN MOVIE:
The Princess Diaries

A CLOTHING ITEM:
Colored Shorts

A FAMOUS LANDMARK:
The Leaning Tower of Pisa

A SEASON:
Spring

AQUARIUS

PERSONALITY TRAITS

AQUARIANS ARE KNOWN for their forward thinking. They often leave their physical states, and that allows for them to dream about every infinite possibility the world has to offer them. Aquarians also represent acceptance, as they are not likely to judge another person for having a different point of view than them. They are wise beyond their years.

They are childlike dreamers who just want to detach from everyday life. However, they also have a very eccentric and erratic quality to their personality. They do not allow for others to tell them how to act and what to do, and they cannot be bogged down by jobs that try to tie them down as well. Instead of being burdened with a silencing job, Aquarians should be appreciated and revered for their imagination.

To Aquarians, joy and bliss are essential to happiness. They despise rejection, as it tends to throw them off and baffle them. Aquarians just want to approach life simply, without conflict, stress, or demand. They promote high ideals and universal truth. They strive to maintain objectivity and can often be accused of being a little too cold.

AQUARIUS

COMPATIBILITY & RELATIONSHIPS

AQUARIANS ARE VERY UNIQUE CREATURES, and they are also extremely intelligent. They are best suited for someone who will make them feel smart. They cannot be with people who make them feel bad for being a dreamer and for loving so deeply. Sagittarius is an amazing match for Aquarius, because they both value big dreams and are adventurous. Sagittarius will think about the future just as much as Aquarius, and they will live a life filled with fun and exploration.

AQUARIUS AND ARIES COMPATIBILITY: These two will get lost in conversation with each other a lot; long into their relationship, they have nights where they stay up until the sunrise talking. They're on the same mental level, and they both have a lot of interests and things that excite them. They'll be able to form a solid foundation of friendship on which to build a relationship.

AQUARIUS AND TAURUS COMPATIBILITY: This is an unlikely pairing of people who see the world very differently. Aquarians' wacky ideas can feel exhausting for Taurus, while Taurus can feel too boring for Aquarius.

AQUARIUS AND GEMINI COMPATIBILITY: These two make better friends than lovers, but they get along swimmingly. They are both exciting people who love to explore new ideas. They have nonstop conversation and keep each other interested in what can be a very passionate relationship.

AQUARIUS AND CANCER COMPATIBILITY: On paper this pairing should do well, but it often feels like something here won't click. The two people understand each other's needs, but they don't move naturally together. Aquarius will seem too removed from their body and emotions to Cancer, and Cancer will seem too needy and emotional for Aquarius.

AQUARIUS AND LEO COMPATIBILITY: Leo and Aquarius get along best in the bedroom, where they are drawn to an exciting, non-vanilla relationship. Outside the bedroom, they have less in common, but if they put work into really getting to know each other, they can form a strong bond as a couple.

AQUARIUS AND VIRGO COMPATIBILITY: Virgo is going to think Aquarius is a bit crazy at first, but in time they will find out they aren't so incompatible after all. Aquarius, for all their wacky ideas, isn't a total mess like Gemini and can take care of themselves. There will be a little spark here, as both people are somewhat foreign and exotic to the other.

AQUARIUS AND LIBRA COMPATIBILITY: These two will have a super-strong mental connection. They'll love making friends at yoga class and hosting brunch complete with a post-brunch meditation. The relationship will feel light even as they have a serious connection, and they'll generally get along well.

AQUARIUS AND SCORPIO COMPATIBILITY: While Scorpio might take things to heart and read people very closely, Aquarius has the ability to brush things off. They will give Scorpio the time they need to come back to them. They will never overwhelm them with attention, and they don't need much themselves beyond the loyalty that comes with being with Scorpio.

AQUARIUS AND SAGITTARIUS COMPATIBILITY: This is a good match, as both signs are curious explorers. They won't hold each other back, and they'll be happy partners exploring ideas and the world together.

AQUARIUS AND CAPRICORN COMPATIBILITY: This is a hard relationship to get going, as they don't live very similar lifestyles. The one thing that could make it work is Capricorn and Aquarius's shared interests in classical ideas—philosophy and art. If they can build a solid foundation of friendship based on common interests, they might begin to understand and meet each other's needs.

AQUARIUS AND AQUARIUS COMPATIBILITY: Aquarians work well with their own sign, as they tend to have pretty high opinions of themselves, so being in a relationship with a person who is similar to them is very helpful. Together they will keep each other mentally stimulated, and their romantic connection will thrive because of this consistent spark.

AQUARIUS AND PISCES COMPATIBILITY: This combination is never boring. This couple goes from one extreme to the other and struggles to find a normal balance together. Pisces constantly seeks love, while Aquarius is naturally distant. Sometimes that works, but other times Pisces will struggle with trust issues, and that's when the two fight. When you're constantly doubting someone, it's never going to work out.

HOW TO ATTRACT AQUARIUS

To attract Aquarius, be simple and free, open-minded, and dreamy. They like it when people do small things for them, so little acts of kindness or small gestures will always go a long way with Aquarius. Ask them about their day, give them your free time, make sure that you plan to see them, and integrate them into even your most normal activities like grocery shopping. Aquarius simply wants to feel like you appreciate their company, and they don't like anything too intense. So attract them lightly and in simplistic ways.

HOW TO KNOW IF AQUARIUS LIKES YOU

If Aquarius likes you, they will want to be around you. They are reserved when it comes to emotions, but they will encourage you to take what you want. Usually, this means them, but they will test you to see if you will be deterred. If you are unsure of Aquarius and have another conquest in mind, they will often tell you that you deserve better than that person. They will always try to steer you in their direction. If Aquarius keeps a conversation going with you for a long period, know that they admire you—Aquarians are very bad at focusing their attention in regular situations.

HOW AQUARIUS IS IN A RELATIONSHIP

In a relationship, Aquarius needs intellectual stimulation. It is what turns them on and keeps them interested in their partner. They adore long chats and love talking about the future, for it gives them something to dream about. When in love, Aquarius needs a very honest and open relationship and cannot hold back their feelings. They need to be able to express themselves. In long-term engagements, Aquarians will nurture a very dynamic, progressive lifestyle, and they will inspire those they love to dream big with them.

IDEAL DATE FOR AQUARIUS

Aquarius often needs a date to be both stimulating and social. A concert would be an amazing mix of those two aspects, and it will also appeal to the Aquarian obsession with live music. Bring your Aquarian to a little jazz club or out to a bar where one of their favorite bands is playing. They will be in heaven, and they will also love that they get to share those moments with you.

HOW AQUARIUS IS IN THE BEDROOM

In the bedroom, Aquarius will always play hard to get. To do the deed, they need to be very mentally stimulated. It takes long conversations and intense situations to get Aquarius to sleep with you. When they decide that you are worthy, they are extremely fun between the sheets. They will joke around in between bouts of intensity. They are also very kinky creatures.

HOW AQUARIUS DEALS WITH HEARTBREAK

Aquarius is never fully emotionally attached in a relationship, so their broken hearts aren't as bad as some others in the zodiac. They do not hurt as deeply. Though they experience feelings of insecurity at first, it usually only takes a day or two for them to realize that they are worthy of much more.

HOW AQUARIUS ARE AS FRIENDS

Aquarius represents friendship in the zodiac. They have a lot of friends, and that is an understatement. They network and they love all forms of social media. They are well-loved by their pals because they have a very unique point of view and a detachment that makes them come off as very cool. Though they do often seem aloof, they are deeply loyal and compassionate friends. They will always notice when someone they care about is struggling, and they will go out of their way to support that person. While social, they also need time alone to recharge and the transition from social to solo time may be abrupt. Don't be surprised if Aquarius is the life of the party one minute, then escaping out the back door the next.

HOW TO GAIN THE RESPECT OF AQUARIANS

In order for Aquarius to respect you, you must agree with them. They admire people who think the same way they do.

HOW AQUARIANS ARE WHEN THEY'RE MAD

When mad, Aquarius will often just stop talking to the person who angered them. They will get into their car or lock themselves away in their room with their favorite music to cool off and feel better. They will purposely try to ignore the source of their anger for as long as possible in the hopes that it will help them calm down. If they can't relax, Aquarius will enter a mode of extreme infuriation, and they will lose their temper. They will unload all of their negative feelings, and it will take a while for them to start talking to that person again after they have blown up.

HOW AQUARIANS ARE WHEN THEY'RE SAD

When sad, Aquarius tends to feel uneasy. They will be hard to reach and will shut down and isolate themselves. They tend to detach when feeling upset, but they will try their best to hide it with a happy, fake disposition. If Aquarius is otherwise healthy but sleeping more than usual, checking out and making excuses to be alone, or overly obsessing about something, they may be sad without even being fully conscious of it.

SIMPLE THINGS THAT MAKE AQUARIUS HAPPY

Aquarius loves reflection, and they adore nights spent listening to good music while thinking about everything on their mind.

AQUARIUS AT THEIR BEST

At their best, Aquarians are strong in their convictions. They have the capacity to change the world with their beliefs and their goals, because they will fight to the end to achieve what they want to achieve. They will always go after what they want and take chances. They are intelligent, goofy, and a giant kid at heart, which makes them extremely charming and lovable.

AQUARIANS AT THEIR WORST

At their worst, Aquarians can come off as intense creeps. They try too hard and often fish for sympathy, attention, and validation. They cannot pick up on social cues and tend to be very invasive without even realizing it. Before they know it, they have often taken things way too far and have upset a lot of people with their mindlessness.

WHAT AQUARIANS FEAR THE MOST

The one thing that Aquarius fears the most would be isolation from their loved ones. They truly hate the idea that one day they could lose those close to them and completely get cut out of the life of someone whom they consider important.

AQUARIUS'S LIKELY OCCUPATIONS

Aquarians are natural-born humanitarians. They are always up for entertaining odd or abnormal ideas, and they have an extremely curious mind. They are bound to end up in an unconventional job and are often pursuing positions they have created for themselves. Aquarians absolutely hate corporate environments, and they need freedom in their job to bring a fresh perspective to the table each week. Highly repetitive work will seem mundane to Aquarians. They have a need to understand, deconstruct, and innovate. They may demonstrate a variety of talents, wear many hats, or have an uncanny ability to meld both left and right brain qualities. Aquarians can be found working in a variety of fields, including the arts and sciences. Aquarius would make an amazing inventor and a kickass musician.

AQUARIUS'S LIKELY HEALTH CONCERNS

Aquarius is ruled by the circulatory system. Poor circulation can cause arthritis, and if Aquarius gets too caught up in being overzealous with work, they can suffer from nervous disorders.

WHERE TO TAKE AQUARIUS ON VACATION

Aquarians are most likely to repeat vacation destinations. If they experienced great insights or creative inspiration in a certain place, you can bet that they will be right back at that spot the next time they get on a plane. They are known to do annual trips and like to keep things simple, so anything that is familiar to them would be an ideal getaway.

AQUARIUS'S LEARNING STYLE

Aquarians need to develop their own approach to learning. They like to invent new ways of obtaining knowledge and will likely invent electronic gadgets to make learning more fun. Aquarians learn about a subject, then go on to completely innovate or reinvent how the subject, or the process around learning the subject, is done. Always thinking on the macro level, Aquarius may quickly grow bored with the smaller details because the big picture is more appealing to them. In other words, they will learn how each smaller piece works so they can better grasp, and very likely reinvent, the whole.

AQUARIUS'S HUMOR

Aquarius is simply funny in a very natural way. They don't try to be a joker or make people laugh, but they do. This bewilders them and often leaves them giggling along out of confusion.

AQUARIUS'S FAVORITE PASTIME

Aquarius adores writing, daydreaming, and sleeping. They are always happy when playing an instrument or listening to music.

WHAT TO SAY TO MOTIVATE YOUR AQUARIUS

No one will ever be able to understand you. This may make you feel alone, confused, or misunderstood, but please—know that it is your greatest asset. You are on a level that no one can reach, and you have the ability to lead and dream and make incredible things happen because you are truly a genius. People are captivated by you. They want to know you. Even if they can't comprehend your mind, they will always be fascinated by it and appreciate it. Keep going; you will do much more standing out than fitting in.

PISCES

DATES	February 18 – March 20
SIGN	Fish
RULING PLANET	Jupiter
ZODIAC QUALITY	Mutable
ELEMENT	Water
POSITIVE TRAITS	Artistic, Loving, Deep
NEGATIVE TRAITS	Overly Sensitive, Lazy, Pessimistic

IF PISCES WAS...

A STARBUCKS DRINK:
White Hot Chocolate

A COLOR:
Grey-Blue

A GREEK GOD:
Hades—god of the underworld

AN ADDICTION:
Alcohol

AN ALCOHOLIC BEVERAGE:
Jack & Coke

A DRUG:
Valium

IN A HIGH-SCHOOL CLIQUE:
Stoner Kids

A CITY:
London, England

A HARRY POTTER HOUSE:
Gryffindor

AN UNTRANSLATABLE FRENCH PHRASE:
L'appel du vide—the sudden urge to jump when standing on a high-rise

A KISS:
Sensual

A TEEN MOVIE:
She's the Man

A CLOTHING ITEM:
Comfortable Leggings

A FAMOUS LANDMARK:
Niagara Falls

A SEASON:
Spring

PISCES

PERSONALITY TRAITS

PISCES ARE CONSIDERED TO BE THE MOST highly evolved sign out of the whole zodiac. They symbolize the human soul, and they have a very deep belief in the universe.

Pisceans swim freely in society and represent the capacity to see the depths of life. They are completely fine with being drowned in the deep end of the world's emotions and offerings, and they are not afraid to simply feel.

There is a dreamy, spiritual, and deeply emotional quality to every Pisces, and resounding sensitivity can make it difficult for these people to lead an easy social life. They are often characterized as the sign of sorrows, for they feel so much and don't often fit in anywhere. They can be vulnerable to depression; occasionally, self-pity and insecurity overcome them. Pisceans are also known for using escapism in the form of drugs to enter into their dream worlds and forget about their woes. Their deep and complex emotional life makes them highly attractive to those who thirst to learn more about opening themselves up.

Pisceans can be very generous and are highly empathic when it comes to the difficulties of others, and they tend to act with compassion in the face of misfortune.

PISCES

COMPATIBILITY & RELATIONSHIPS

PISCES ARE DREAMY AND EMPATHETIC. They are sensitive, in-decisive, and need affection. Pisces needs to find a partner that will nurture their unique approach to relationships. They will need to commit to some-one who will be able to brighten them up when they get in their heads. Pisces will always find a great partner in someone who will accept and appreciate their love, for it is so rare and needs to be protected. Scorpio will do just that, falling in love with how Pisces meets their depths perfectly.

PISCES AND ARIES COMPATIBILITY: This combination isn't the strongest, as they struggle in communication. Pisces might drop hints about what they want and need, but they will never straight-up say it. Aries needs that clarity which they don't get. In a relationship with Pisces, one has to be able to read people very well, but with Aries they seem to overlook that. This couple fails because each person just can't figure out or fake being what the other person needs.

PISCES AND TAURUS COMPATIBILITY: This is a wonderful match pairing a dreamer (Pisces) with a realist (Taurus). They both prefer a laid-back lifestyle and know the other person needs to be supported and loved. They will have one of the happiest home lives and be a couple with an un-shakable bond.

PISCES AND GEMINI COMPATIBILITY: Gemini + Pisces balance each other out very well. While Pisces is very emotional and deep, Geminis are very compassionate and understanding of their needs. Pisces has no shame in being exactly who they are and following how they feel, while Gemini tends to play the role of what someone needs them to be and makes the choices that seem logical. What each side needs, the other seems to be.

PISCES AND CANCER COMPATIBILITY: Cancer and Pisces will fundamentally understand each other, but they're so similar that they will have a hard time functioning in the real world as a couple. Both of these signs work best when they're paired with a sturdier person who lives in the real world—not another dreamer. This point aside, they will be perfectly happy together and will create a beautiful, creative world where everyone is nice to each other and the world is made up of art.

PISCES AND LEO COMPATIBILITY: In this relationship, Leo has to be the strong and stable one. Pisces are very needy in relationships. Because everything in Pisces's life is based on how they feel, they need a partner who understands and can nurture that. Where Pisces might lack confidence, Leo always is the confident one. Where Pisces might crumble, Leo has no problem being their strength. This couple is good together when each person understands the role they play, but problems occur most of the time when being the strong one becomes too much for Leo.

PISCES AND VIRGO COMPATIBILITY: This combination is the relationship every parent wants their kids to be in. It's a practical relationship that creates a down-to-earth and productive duo. While it might not be that love story that keeps you up at night, they are the love you know will be loyal and someone who will keep their vows if ever you choose each other.

PISCES AND LIBRA COMPATIBILITY: This pair is one of the strongest. Their loyalty to one another is what is so great. They each are empathetic and would give anyone the shirt off their back. They make such a good team because when one is down the other steps up when they need to, and vice versa. This relationship is a forever combination if you're lucky to find such a thing. And together it isn't so much that each person completes each other; who they are is a reflection of the influence they have on each other.

PISCES AND SCORPIO COMPATIBILITY: Opposites attract. Scorpio can be cold or guarded. They struggle in trusting people and letting anyone in. They always want to be the dominant one in a relationship. Pisces, on the other hand, tends to be passive, wearing their heart on their sleeve and loving Scorpio as hard as they possibly can. A high level of honesty will be required to make this combination work, but it may also feel smothering for Pisces to meet the high expectations of honesty and devotion set by Scorpio. While it's likely to be a challenge, once they have Scorpio's trust, what makes this bond so strong is their loyalty to one another.

PISCES AND SAGITTARIUS COMPATIBILITY: Emotionally this combination balances each other out very well. They each are hopeless romantics and wear their heart on their sleeve, and they respect that about each other. They are empathetic and understanding and truly vibe with what each is feeling and trying to be what each person needs in the relationship. The only problem that occurs in this type of relationship is the level of intense emotions between the two is sometimes too dramatic; they need someone a little bit different.

PISCES AND CAPRICORN COMPATIBILITY: This pair is one that probably started off as friends first, each wondering who was gonna make the first move and when. Any relationship that starts as a friendship you know will be one that's loyal and long-lasting. It's the relationship that comes into one another's lives when everyone is tired of getting hurt and played. It's the relationship that makes them feel safe and secure.

PISCES AND AQUARIUS COMPATIBILITY: This combination is never boring. This couple goes from one extreme to the other, and they struggle to find a normal balance together. Pisces constantly seeks love, while Aquarius is naturally distant. And sometimes that works, but other times Pisces struggles with trust issues and that's when the two fight. When you're constantly doubting someone, it's never going to work out.

PISCES AND PISCES COMPATIBILITY: The combination of two Pisces is horrifyingly strong and compatible. They find each other, and each feels like they found their soul mate or the missing parts of who they need in another person. The relationship takes off almost instantly, and that's what scares each of them and might drive them away from each other. It's finding that person who is perfect for you, but the next question they each have to ask themselves is, "Are you ready for that sort of thing yet?"

HOW TO ATTRACT PISCES

To attract Pisces, buy them something meaningful or make them something that holds merit with them. If you know what they like, use that for your gifts. Whenever they use that gift, they will think about you and be reminded of how thoughtful you are. Make them dinner, write them a letter—Pisces simply wants to know that you are thinking of them and that you understand them.

HOW TO KNOW IF PISCES LIKES YOU

If Pisces likes you, they get very coy and very silly. They are dreamers, and they will always want to share their craziest fantasies and desires with you. Their awkwardness is often very endearing, and their fits of laughter are a telltale sign that they find you charming. If Pisces likes you, it will feel like you are in high school again. They will poke you and giggle a lot, and they will approach you in childish ways, sending cute text messages and flirty comments your way. If Pisces flirts with you more online versus in person, just know that this is because they are shy and tend to withdraw in real-life situations. This does not mean that they don't like you or that they're playing games. They're just more confident online.

HOW PISCES ARE IN A RELATIONSHIP

In a relationship, Pisces is an extreme romantic. They are loving, tender, and very generous with their heart. They adore intimacy. They are very deep beings, and therefore they do not waste their time with flings and superficial relationships. Pisces needs depth, and they need to be appreciated for their sensitivity and their doting loyalty. They fall in love hard, and they will do absolutely anything for their partners. They are truly the most chivalrous sign of the zodiac, and loving them is a beautiful experience.

IDEAL DATE FOR PISCES

For Pisces, expression is really important. Appeal to their creative side and their appreciation of the arts by bringing them to a local art battle or a place where they can paint and drink a few beverages. They will love watching you channel your inner creative, and they will feel energized and inspired in the environment.

HOW PISCES ARE IN THE BEDROOM

Pisces will couple sex and love. They go hand-in-hand for these sensitive souls. In bed, Pisces loves to be emotionally stimulated, complimented, and kissed deeply. They need to feel comfortable and will only open up when they feel secure with their lovers.

HOW PISCES DEALS WITH HEARTBREAK

When dealing with heartbreak, Pisces will often resort to self-pity. They will feel heartbreak in full force, and they will often succumb to their insecurities. They will convince themselves that they were not good enough and that they drove their past love away. In order to cope with the intensity of their sadness, Pisces will isolate themselves and revel in their dream world until someone comes along to fill their heart with excitement and hope again.

HOW PISCEANS ARE AS FRIENDS

As a friend, Pisces is a very compassionate source of love for others. They help anyone in need and are often taken advantage of because of how willing they are to stick their neck out for others. Their kind nature is either extremely appreciated or completely taken for granted. Therefore, Pisces tends to pick and choose friends with a lot of reservation. They may be guarded at first because they have been so hurt by fake pals in the past. Due to their close-knit choices, Pisces will stick to childhood friends who understand their depth. That way they won't have to worry about being hurt, and they will never have to explain their dispositions or their depth. Pisces truly believe in the saying, "No new friends."

HOW TO GAIN THE RESPECT OF PISCES

To gain the respect of Pisces, all you have to do is simply be a nice person. They really admire creative types who are also affectionate and deep.

HOW PISCES ARE WHEN THEY'RE MAD

Due to constantly feeling so deeply, it is difficult for Pisces to get mad. They often have worked through everything time and time again and have been able to experience and feel through whatever it was that angered them. When they do lash out, it is never on others. Rather, Pisces is known for being very self-destructive, and they will get aggressive with themselves. After an episode, Pisces will need a lot of time to reenergize their heart and feel dreamy again.

HOW PISCES ARE WHEN THEY'RE SAD

When sad, Pisces will suffer from anxiety. They will isolate themselves, and they will feel their sadness in an extremely intense manner. They will ruminate over the situation that is upsetting them, and they will cry about every bad thing that has ever happened to them, even if those situations are irrelevant to them at that given moment.

SIMPLE THINGS THAT MAKE PISCES HAPPY

Pisces love movies and closeness. Nothing beats cuddling for Pisces, and they adore being next to someone who truly gets them.

PISCES AT THEIR BEST

At their best, Pisces are filled with such a beautiful capacity to nurture and feel. They are caretakers and will do anything to show you that they are there for you. They treat everyone as their equal, and they are cheerful and inspiring people. They are fun, kind, and they will always treat people the way they want to be treated. Pisces often need to be protected; that is how rare and stunning their hearts are.

PISCES AT THEIR WORST

At their worst, Pisces will take things way too seriously, and they will go to extremes emotionally. They can be reckless, self-destructive, and their need to escape upsetting situations often causes them to isolate themselves and hide without ever taking responsibility for their actions.

WHAT PISCES FEAR THE MOST

To creative and sensitive Pisces, criticism is a terrible thing. They fear confrontation to the point of needing to run away from it to avoid being called out or hurt. They simply cannot handle judgment.

PISCES'S LIKELY OCCUPATIONS

Pisces are old souls. They are creative, passionate, and they excel at traditional jobs in the arts. They make amazing musicians, dancers, and photographers. Pisceans are very intuitive, and when that is added into a creative, service-oriented job, the results are incredible. People really feel understood and listened to when it comes to being served by Pisces. Other than that, Pisceans would make incredible philanthropists, veterinarians, and psychologists, because they foster a lot of compassion within their big hearts.

PISCES'S LIKELY HEALTH CONCERNS

Pisceans are often associated with the feet and the lymphatic system. Pisces must allow for ample dreaming time and rest, or else their immune system will grow to be combative and problematic.

WHERE TO TAKE PISCES ON VACATION

Pisces are quite easily pleased when it comes to vacations. All they need is a beach, a comfy place to rest, and an amazing view. An island is always a good idea, because Pisces are known to be water babies. They love being surrounded by the ocean's depths.

PISCES'S LEARNING STYLE

Pisces learns in both an emotional and sensitive way. They gain their knowledge and their experience through daydreaming. They often need teachers that will be patient with them and seek tutors that create a safe place for their creative thinking.

PISCES'S HUMOR

Pisces will either tell cute, funny stories, or they will be obnoxious with their humor. It is very easy for them to get carried away and spend an hour telling something that loses its comedic appeal very quickly.

PISCES'S FAVORITE PASTIME

Pisces love video gaming and listening to music. Their favorite thing to do, however, is to daydream.

WHAT TO SAY TO MOTIVATE YOUR PISCES

You are the most beautiful soul—the perfect balance of sensitivity and mind. You will always get what you want if you simply focus and trust that you are worthy of success. Keep focusing on the positive. Don't let the world hang heavy on your shoulders. You are allowed to put your load down. You are incredible, and you truly need to see that. You are worthy of so much—repeat that, and keep on repeating that until you truly believe it.

Here's What You Need To Cut Out Of Your Life

BASED ON YOUR ZODIAC SIGN

ARIES

Aries are adventurous and independent. They have no problem going on a solo expedition into the unknown. However, they struggle with the routine and focus on what is necessary to achieve their major life goals. Aries need to give up the idea that life is supposed to be a nonstop movie montage where each day is different and more exciting than the last. Learn to find joy in the new adventures you're able to experience as a result of sticking around for a while.

TAURUS

Every Taurus needs to cut out of their life the belief that everyone who tries to get close to them is out to tame them or force them to give up the independence they love so much. It's very possible for someone to love you as you are without needing to own or change you. Be open to people.

GEMINI

Geminis notoriously have a hard time making up their mind.

They want to pursue every project they think of. They pick up and drop hobbies and dreams like other people change clothes. To grow, Geminis need to let go of the guilt they hang onto about being fickle. Sure, it seems flaky, but it stems from their biggest strength: zest for life. Who cares what other people think? Be happy with your energetic, lively, creative self.

CANCER
Cancers have an incredible capacity to love people, but with that comes the capacity to be hurt. A lot. Cancers need to let go of the people in their past who didn't love them and look to the future when they will find someone who will.

LEO
Leos need to let go of the need to be praised by others in order to feel confident in themselves. This is a nice way to receive affection, but it can't be a requirement for the world to always approve of you.

VIRGO
Virgos need to give up the belief that everything has to be planned and ordered before it can be perfect. A little spontaneity is healthy for you! Be your put-together self *most* of the time, but when the opportunity presents itself, learn to be a teeny-tiny bit reckless.

LIBRA
Libras need to learn to let go of the weight of other people's feelings. Libras take on other people's emotional needs freely: They love to help their loved ones solve problems by being their logical yet empathetic sounding board. While a good trait, it can be very draining. At the end of the day, they need to let go of this burden and worry about their own self-care.

SCORPIO
Scorpios need to give up the need to be right all the time. They get caught up in trying to "win" arguments at any cost and end

up hurting the people they care about. Mature Scorpios realize they don't have to react to everything and that sometimes it's more important to find consensus than to be right.

SAGITTARIUS

Sagittarius people need to cut out extra flirting. It's hard to give up something you get an ego boost from, but past a certain point it's not fair to the emotions of those hearts you're stringing along.

CAPRICORN

Capricorns need to cut back on their cold exterior shell. Every single relationship in Capricorn's life will be better if they make just a small effort on this front. People aren't out to get you; it will be okay to let them in a little bit.

AQUARIUS

Aquarians need to give up the feeling that everyone should care as much as they do. It's your gift, Aquarius! It wouldn't be as special if we were all exactly the same.

PISCES

Pisces need to ease up on the self-doubt. It's a hard thing to cut out completely, especially for such creative people, but they truly have an abundance of it. Keep a journal of nice things people say about you and reference it when you're feeling down. Everyone loves Pisces!

Why Everyone Is Jealous Of You

BASED ON YOUR ZODIAC SIGN

 ### ARIES
You will never get into a Netflix-and-chill rut with Aries. They are exciting, adventurous, and always trying new things. They have the energy most of us crave—and the charm to not feel awkward about trying something where you have to meet a bunch of new people.

 ### TAURUS
You don't give a fuck what anyone thinks. A lot of people say this, but you actually *mean* it. You're an individual, and you get to do whatever you want without waiting around for people's approval.

 ### GEMINI
You have an energetic charm that makes people want to bet on you and your ideas. You're bright and creative—and unlike every other kind of creative person, you know how to sell your ideas so you can actually *make something* from them.

CANCER

Cancers have an incredible capacity to love. No one will love you as deeply and completely as Cancer will love you. They are feared by exes who secretly know their ex is happier and healthier with a Cancerian partner.

LEO

Nice guys and girls everywhere bitterly envy Leo who has no problem singing their own praises. Leos are successful and get their well-deserved acclaim because, very simply, they ask for it. In their own subtle way, they are masters of never letting anyone walk all over them or letting their hard work go unnoticed.

VIRGO

Virgos are some put-together bitches. No one can solve a problem like Virgo can, which is why everyone wants them on their team. They are sought-after friends, employees, and even romantic partners for this reason.

LIBRA

People are jealous of Libras because they always have so many friends. And *good* friends, too. They are social in the perfect way—charming enough to have a lot of friends, but gracious enough to make each one of them feel loved.

SCORPIO

You're feisty and passionate and no one will ever be able to describe you as passive. Everyone else wishes they had the spring in their step that you do. Even when they care about something, it doesn't come with the truckload of energy and focus it does for you.

SAGITTARIUS

Sagittarians are *really* funny. They have the ability to be irreverent and "go there" without pissing anybody off. We're all a little jealous of how Sagittarius can make us laugh.

CAPRICORN

Capricorns are stoic and strong. We're jealous of their ability to be assholes. This sounds like a negative factor, but it's truly a gift: Capricorn never goes to bed wanting. They get ahead and live enviable lives because they know what they want and get after it.

AQUARIUS

Aquarians are activists and allies. They vote, they volunteer, they go vegan, and they genuinely care much more than most people. They're the person other people say they want to be but aren't.

PISCES

Pisces have minds we remember generations later. They are artists, and even if we don't notice them right away due to their quiet and laid-back nature, sooner or later we'll be blown away by the way they see the world.

The Unedited Truth About Why You Suck

BASED ON YOUR ZODIAC SIGN

ARIES

You are insensitive, crabby, and volatile. It's like one minute everything is great, and then MOOD SWING and you're sulking for the rest of the day. Every Aries needs to immediately learn to deal with their feelings, but you all claim you aren't emotional people.

TAURUS

You think the world is only about you. It's insufferable to be in a relationship with Taurus—friendship, romantic, or otherwise—because you fundamentally view others negatively. You're paranoid that others are trying to infringe on your independence when all they probably want is to, like, chill.

GEMINI

You need to decide which personality you have and then stick with it. It's hard to take you seriously when you are a new person every week and have the focus of a toddler. Most people aren't looking to parent an adult child.

CANCER

You cry too much, and it makes people uncomfortable. You're an absolute baby when you feel hurt or sad or things don't go your way. Also, if you're SO SENSITIVE AND EMOTIONALLY DEEP, maybe you should use some of your powers to tell people how you feel instead of making us guess.

LEO

Leos are sooooo exhaustingly thirsty for praise. I wish I could go back in time and make your mom hug you more. It's claustrophobic being around you, because you need me to notice and affirm every tiny thing. You need to learn how to love yourself.

VIRGO

You nag. You care too much about tiny details. You're boring. You always have to be right.

LIBRA

Libras think they are the voice of God when it comes to making a "balanced" and "reasonable" decision. It sucks to date/be friends with you, when all you care about is logic and not the individual people involved in the decision. Sometimes it's okay to prioritize your inner circle.

SCORPIO

Your ego is so incredibly massive that anyone who chooses to love a Scorpio does so knowing they will have to deal with wrestling it the rest of their life. Sometimes it's just not that deep and you're left being embarrassed you're with the aggro bro/chick.

SAGITTARIUS

Sagittarians are narcissistic children who need everyone to tell them how cool they are. You worship travel YouTubers but insist you could do it better. You have guy-who-hangs-out-at-high-school-after-he-graduates energy.

CAPRICORN

You come off as soulless in a boring way—villains such as your-self should at least be interesting. Also, you are impressively bad at sex. Sorry.

AQUARIUS

All Aquarians kinda give off Charles Manson vibes.

PISCES

You smell like weed and are constantly bumming people out.

What You Need To Overcome In Order To Find Love

BASED ON YOUR ZODIAC SIGN

ARIES

Aries are confident and gregarious. You thrive on challenges and draw people to you with your charm. The downside of this is that you sometimes steamroll your partner, especially if you are with a quieter, less short-tempered sign.

You might wonder why your relationships seem to end so suddenly when you thought things were going (mostly) well. To reverse this trend, you need to learn to be quiet and listen sometimes. Master the art of <u>deep listening</u>. Take time to *really hear* what your partner is saying about their needs, and slow down long enough to make sure you are giving it to them. Try to walk together instead of leading.

TAURUS

Taurus is a sign that's always being made aware of your major flaw: stubbornness. It's something we associate with Taurus people more often than all their gifts: You make incredible friends. You are loyal, interesting, generous, and deep people.

When you are with someone, you are truly a *partner* in every sense of the word.

But yes, you are overly stubborn and hate when you have to give up your independence. And you can be lazy. In order for Taurus to find love, you have to decide that you really want it and then appeal to your finely tuned logic to understand you have to open up. Other people are not the enemy. Potential dates are not trying to steal something from you or make your life more inefficient. You are going to have to experience normal bumps in the road, and you have to decide it's worth it—or be content being single.

GEMINI

Geminis are energetic and imaginative. You never lose your sense of childlike wonder and are happy to be constantly learning and discovering new things about the world.

But I can't overstate how much you struggle with commitment.

It's not because Geminis are bad people; it's just that it's harder than usual for you to figure out what you want. How can you commit to something if you aren't sure you will want it tomorrow? For Gemini to find love, you have to tackle your restlessness. A good way to do this is to make sure an adventurous spirit is on your "have to have" list. Focus on finding someone who has as much wanderlust as you, someone for whom commitment doesn't mean slowing down, but having a partner to move with.

CANCER

Cancer will be the best boyfriend or girlfriend your partner will ever have as long as you don't smother them to death in the process. You are incredibly loving, romantic, and generous with your time, money, and heart. You will try your hardest to make sure your partner is happy and feels loved at all times.

However, you need to spend time working on yourself and maturing before you get into a relationship. If you jump in before you have learned to be confident in yourself, you become insecure and overly needy when it comes to your partner's praise and affection. And when you don't get it, you sulk instead of communicating.

It's really only because you give so much of yourself in a relationship that they ask you to take this extra time to make sure you are ready to be healthy in one. You don't casually date, and so the intensity of your love requires preliminary work.

LEO

You are creative and driven. You are generally smarter than average and typically become successful. What you struggle with is getting the recognition you need for your talents. Because of this, you prefer relationships to being single, even if the relationship leaves much to be desired.

Your biggest love obstacle is holding out and not settling. You need to surround yourself with a support system of friends and family who validate you until you find someone truly worth building a relationship with.

VIRGO

Hardworking and practical, you make a great partner for almost anyone. People like to have you in their life because you always add value to it by being the one who will make plans, find the best restaurants, fix their budget, and figure out how to maximize every area of life.

The main problem you have in love is getting out of your shell and comfort zone long enough to meet the right person. It's easy for Virgo to get into a routine and be perfectly happy to do the same things with the same people. But love requires work and vulnerability. Find an extroverted Gemini or Aries to introduce you to some new activities and potential love interests.

LIBRA

Gracious and diplomatic, you almost always possess a high social IQ. You are incredibly skilled at making and keeping relationships, so why do you struggle with finding The One?

You dislike confrontation and can carry a grudge.

This is a good quality disguised as a bad quality; you simply want your relationship to be harmonious. You need to learn that in order to be happy, you need to bite the bullet and confront issues head-on. Don't let it build up until you are past the point of no return. Those conversations will never be as hard in real life as you think they will be in your head, and you'll save yourself a lot of time and frustration.

SCORPIO

You are the kind of person that tends to be either loved or hated—rare is the person who has lukewarm feelings about Scorpio. Confident and passionate, you are champions of the people you love and feared by the people you hate. You also tend to be the best sex partner in the zodiac.

Your fatal relationship flaw, however, is this same passion. You can be jealous, obsessive, and manipulative. You need to be right, you need to win every argument, and you need to be not just loved but *revered* by your partner. It's a lot.

In order to move forward and find a healthy, lasting relationship, you need to focus on finding someone who will balance out your personality, not challenge it. Fellow water signs Pisces and Cancer are good places to start. They have no issues opening up and being vulnerable, so there's no need for Scorpio's jealousy to make an appearance. You will feel secure in the love you are receiving and meet your potential as a partner.

SAGITTARIUS

You will generally be the funniest person in your social circle, so you don't have a problem attracting people into your life. You are fun-loving and adventurous but without the accompanying flaw of being restless and unhappy when you aren't constantly stimulated.

The problem is that along with this humor and gregariousness can be a lack of tact that puts people off—especially between Sagittarius men and women and more sensitive signs. It's far too easy for a well-meaning Sagittarius to hurt someone unintentionally. What's fair game for you is too far for others.

You either need to wait around for someone with thick skin or learn to increase the amount of assurance and affection you give your partner so that these minor misunderstandings don't keep ending potentially good relationships.

CAPRICORN

You are independent and adept. People like you because you are smart and usually successful. You know how to work hard and achieve what you want.

In love, however, you are less adept. You are cold and nagging, and dating Capricorn can get boring. You need to learn how to be more imaginative, more open, and less inhibited. When in a relationship, consider keeping the spark alive. Part of the work of being successful there is to treat it like a business opportunity and schedule exciting dates and nights to try new things with your loved one.

AQUARIUS

Smart, funny, and completely original, you are a compelling individual. You lead nonprofits, become politicians, write life-changing books—you inspire everyone else to be better. But this doesn't make you good at relationships.

You are your own biggest obstacle on the road to love. You dislike emotional expression and can feel trapped in the confines of commitment. In order to get a relationship to work, you need to be with someone who won't smother you, who will encourage you to be as independent as you desire and won't feel insecure about it.

You should only be willing to date other deeply individual and independent people. You should select deep thinkers who are too wise to be thrown off by the lack of affection that might accompany an important work project or an election. Sagittarius or Gemini will solve this problem.

PISCES

Compassionate, loving, and devoted, you are a sought-after partner—when you are bold enough to make other people realize how valuable you are. While you possess myriad qualities that make you desirable, you can also be shy and meek, so those qualities go unnoticed.

To find success in love, all you need to do is resolve to have a little more courage and a little less patience. Learn the art of a good brag once in a while. Don't let people pass you up for the very fixable reason that they just haven't heard how great you are.

This Is How You Attract People

BASED ON YOUR ZODIAC SIGN

 ### ARIES

We are drawn to Aries people because they always seem so confident in what they are doing. While they may have inner doubt, they present an aspirational I-know-what-I'm-doing vibe to those around them. Unlike most other signs, they embrace change, adventure, and the unknown. They make amazing partners whether romantic, platonic, or professional because they will take you out of your rut and into something much more exciting.

TAURUS

We are drawn to Taurus people because they don't take shit from anyone. While some of us may prefer to avoid conflict or assume people mistreating us is "not a big deal," Taurus will make a scene and demand the respect they (and their friends) deserve. They are extremely warm-hearted to those who have earned a place in their heart, and they inspire all of us to fiercely protect our loved ones.

GEMINI

We are drawn to Geminis because they are not afraid of their idiosyncrasies. They contradict themselves all the time, and they are stronger for it. They aren't afraid to admit when they are wrong, because they are changing their mind all the time. This results in open-minded individuals who can talk about any subject on the planet, because they've been interested in it at one time or another. They make the best dinner party guests in the zodiac.

CANCER

We are drawn to Cancers because they are supremely loving and sensitive individuals. They are romantics who produce amazing literature and art—or even just a beautifully designed home. They are picky about experiences and aesthetics, so when you are with Cancer, each event will feel special—even a night home watching Netflix on the couch.

LEO

We are drawn to Leos because they are creative performers. They are always hysterical, always the favorite friend of the group, always the person who entertains you and creates the best memories. They are the opposite of dull, and they punctuate your relationship with quality LOLs.

VIRGO

We are drawn to Virgos because they make us better people. They show us that "adulting" isn't actually that hard. Life is better without the drama of procrastination or keeping your bank account unbalanced. They are the friends and romantic partners our parents wish we would have, the ones that leave our lives in better shape than they found it.

LIBRA

We are drawn to Libras because they are the ultimate listening ear. They are our dream shoulder to cry on, because they can objectively evaluate any situation and give amazing advice. They are the person who helps you write the email to smooth out a friendship or a wrinkle in a work relationship. They are the perfect partner for planning to make any situation better.

SCORPIO

We are drawn to Scorpios because they are intense in the most intoxicating way. They turn monotasking into an art form. If you can capture Scorpio, you will know what it's like to be the focus of someone's complete attention—and be able to watch them as they just *kill* their personal and professional ambitions with this same drive.

SAGITTARIUS

We are drawn to Sagittarians because they let us embrace our inner basic bitch with no judgment. *Sweatpants, hair tied, chillin' with no makeup on, that's when you the prettiest...* We can all let go and indulge in our base desires with our Sag friends. They are a vacation in human form.

CAPRICORN

We are drawn to Capricorns because no one can gossip like Capricorns can. If you are in the mood to shit-talk someone, you will never find a better outlet or a sharper-tongued conversation partner. They are judgmental and have sky-high standards, and sometimes this is exactly what you need.

AQUARIUS

We are drawn to Aquarians because they have magnetic personalities. They are fundamentally open people who are up for new experiences and ways of thinking. They are original and interesting and will consistently introduce you to new things you end up adopting as part of your own interests.

PISCES

We are drawn to Pisces people because they are the quiet sidekick we all are desperate for. They make us feel like stars and secure in their dependable, loyal love. They are sensitive, loving people who care deeply about their relationships without ever being showy or dramatic about it. We should all be so lucky to count them as our loved one.

Here's What Kind Of Girlfriend You Are

BASED ON YOUR ZODIAC SIGN

ARIES

You are the adventurous girlfriend. You are the active, fearless girlfriend who will always be a little bit too much for anyone with homebody tendencies. You're not foolish about rushing into love, but you aren't afraid of it, either. Once you decide you like someone, you see no reason to be coy about it—you're ready to go full speed ahead.

TAURUS

You are the hard-to-get girlfriend. The most appealing guy in the world couldn't get Taurus to open up right away. You don't do one-night stands—not because you don't appreciate sex, but because you'd rather spend time with yourself or your inner circle. You are not down to waste time and vulnerability on someone who hasn't proven themselves to you.

GEMINI

You are the passionate girlfriend. People look at you in amazement because you manage to get *so* excited about *so* many things. You create a life with your partner where there's never a dull moment. No week with you is exactly the same.

CANCER

You are the loving, supportive girlfriend. No one knows what it's like to experience deep, unconditional love until they have been loved by a Cancerian woman. You go out of your way every day to make sure your partner feels loved and supported by you. It's hard for them to move on to their next relationship because they have been spoiled by how good you make them feel.

LEO

You are the flashy girlfriend. Because you love the positive feeling of looking and being desirable, you make it a habit to be this way all the time. Some people might call it high maintenance, but there's a reason people go for that kind of girl—it's exciting! You're the kind of girl people are always curious about because they seem so otherworldly. Dating you will always feel like being an insider to an exclusive club.

VIRGO

You are the stable partner-in-crime girlfriend. When someone gets serious about thinking about who they want to grow old with, they picture Virgo. Virgo has their shit together. They have a good job, they're awesome with money, they're not dramatic—and they're the kind of person everyone runs to with their problems.

LIBRA

You are the power-couple girlfriend. Your social skills are unmatched, and you're warm and loving toward everyone you meet, winning them all over. Libra is the girl a man will seek out when he wants a partner in his ambitious plans, because he knows what a valuable asset she can be in getting close to the right people.

SCORPIO

You are the bombshell girlfriend. No one does sex like Scorpio. It can even be too much for a guy to handle. Because Scorpios are sensual, intense, and confident, they make unforgettable lovers. To them, every relationship revolves around the fun game of sexuality.

SAGITTARIUS

You are the funny-as-hell girlfriend. No one can make you laugh like Sagittarius. They'll ham it up in any situation. They make life better because they never take anything too seriously, including your relationship with them. Sagittarian girls will be with you through thick and thin, making it all feel like an enjoyable adventure.

CAPRICORN

You are the old-fashioned girlfriend. Capricorn women can be considered "cold," but that's only because they're too mature for the heart-on-your-sleeve style of most modern women. They're conservative in a good way—classy, someone who demands you pay them the respect they deserve, without ever uttering a word.

AQUARIUS

You are the charismatic girlfriend. You are filled with passion and enough charisma to convince anyone to be just as passionate about your cause as you are. When the cause is a relationship, you show your partner a world of possibility about what the two of you can do together. You might be loved or hated, but it's very rare for anyone to feel lackluster about you.

PISCES

You are the old-soul girlfriend. You're a renaissance woman who appreciates the classics: good food, good books, beautiful art, and intelligent conversation. You tend to attract other old souls who appreciate your maturity. You need someone who knows there's more to life than sports or video games.

The Unedited Truth About Whether He Really Likes You

BASED ON HIS ZODIAC SIGN

ARIES

If Aries really cares about you, he'll pause to consider your comfort zone. Typically super-independent, they rush into an adventure or a challenge with a "you snooze, you lose" type attitude. But when Aries cares about someone, they make room for them and plan around the fact that just about everyone on Earth is slightly more cautious than they are. You'll be included in event planning and they'll check in with you throughout whatever you're doing to make sure you're comfortable.

TAURUS

There are a lot of ways to tell Taurus *doesn't* love you—they're very judicious about how they spend what little affection they are willing to give. If they open up to you and let themselves be vulnerable when they don't have to, that's how you know Taurus really likes you. They'll make plans with you, invite you into their precious home space, and treat you like you're part of their inner circle.

GEMINI

If Gemini really likes you, he'll stick around through a long period of time. Geminis have a short attention span. It takes a big hook to keep them interested in the same thing week after week when there are so many other bright, shiny objects to chase after. If it's been months and he's still consistent in the attention he gives you, that's when you know Gemini has it for you.

CANCER

Cancers tend to be loving and nurturing toward a lot of people, so you have to figure out if they are showing you a special kind of attention. For Cancers, this tends to involve letting you into the very center of their being: their home. They'll take you to meet their family, try to make your home more comfortable, and cook for you.

LEO

Leos love praise and attention from everyone, so it isn't necessarily special if they preen or perform for you. What's special is the way they go about it. Do they just want you to think they're attractive? Or do they want you to praise them on their ability to keep a nice home, their relationships with their family, or anything else that screams long-term material? If they really like you, they'll want the *right* kind of attention from you.

VIRGO

Virgos are the best at upgrading everyday life. They know the little hacks to make their own lives run seamlessly so they can enjoy success and leisure. If Virgo likes you, they'll turn this trait onto you. All of a sudden, they're helping you automate your bills and signing you up for a CSA box. They make a genuine effort to care for you in very practical ways.

LIBRA

Libras have amazing social skills, so it's easy to feel like they're interested in you. But beware: More than any other sign, Libras plant false flags where they aren't really interested. They just want people to feel good! What separates out the people Libra are *really* interested in is that they're willing to go through a conflict with you. Libras hate conflict, but they're smart enough to know it's necessary in any healthy relationship, so if they bring up some uncomfortable truths and try to sort them out with you, it's real.

SCORPIO

More than any other sign, the old adage is true: If he likes you, you'll *know* he likes you. Scorpios aren't shy or reserved; they believe in taking a risk and making a stand. If you want to know you're not just another notch in their bedpost, wait for them to be a little bit selfless. This is the *last* thing Scorpio wants to do. It comes very unnaturally for them, but that's how you know you mean a lot.

SAGITTARIUS

Sagittarians will flirt with anyone for the fun of it. They are hunters and they love the chase. You'll know you're special when they drop the pretense of the chase: They talk about the future with you, they're unafraid of an Instagram pic that looks like a #coupleselfie, and they show up for the events that aren't necessarily fun for them.

CAPRICORN

They'll do something sweet. Capricorns aren't sentimental by nature, so if they are doing something sappy, they truly believe in the cause. Bonus points if this plan involves them being less than the put-together perfect facade-bot they like to portray.

AQUARIUS

While Aquarians love to understand the emotions of others, they are slow to express their own. They'll ask deep questions of any-one and everyone, but they'll only answer for those they deem worthy. When one has real feelings for you, he will show you the things that are important to his heart. He'll be vulnerable, he'll communicate—you'll feel like there's no barrier between the two of you. For this guy, being on the same philosophical page is extremely important. Your conversations will be deep and probing.

PISCES

You'll be their muse. Pisces are a deeply creative sign. Whatever your man's craft is, you'll be at the center of it. It may not be as literal as his writing love poems about you; maybe he names a batch of his home brew after you. But with this man, know that expressing himself to you will always be important.

The Bitter Truth About Why He Was A Shitty Boyfriend

BASED ON HIS ZODIAC SIGN

ARIES

He always thought he was better than you. Aries are alphas—they are confident, adventurous, and unafraid. Unfortunately, this means they often come with a superiority complex. They look at themselves and what they've done and can't fathom why anyone else would have done less than that. They don't understand the nuances of other people wanting different things than they do. You deserve someone who comes from a place of understanding, not judgment.

TAURUS

He never really let you in. People born under Taurus are strong and steady—which makes them super-attractive, but they can be great big babies about the possibility of getting hurt. They live in paranoia about people wanting to take their independence from them so they pull away, guard their space, and straight-up refuse to get vulnerable. You deserve someone without this baggage who will be an equal partner in emotionally supporting you.

GEMINI

He had shiny-object syndrome. When you met, he lavished you with attention and probably won you over with how much he wanted to be with you. But his affection waned, and you can see him treating new friends the way he used to treat you. You tried everything to get things back to the way they were in the beginning, but there's always going to be someone new on whom they'd rather focus their attention. You deserve someone with an attention span longer than a few weeks.

CANCER

He was too moody for you. Instead of communicating his feelings to you like a grownup, he silently placed expectations on you and then judged you every time you fell short. It's like he was *looking* for reasons to believe you loved him less than he loved you. You deserve love without a scoreboard.

LEO

He needed attention from other women (gross). All Leos need attention and affirmation, but mature Leos can channel it into getting affection from their partner and the people close to them. Immature Leos are slutty flirts who engage with *anyone* of the opposite sex for that sweet hit of attention. No one deserves to have to deal with someone who doesn't view their love as enough.

VIRGO

He was too critical of your shortcomings. Regular people understand that humans are fallible and that we make mistakes. Virgos can be on the extreme end of not understanding this. They are perfectionists, and not just with themselves. It's one thing to be put-together and hold yourself to a higher standard, and it's quite another to inflict that on other people. You deserve someone who understands the importance of grace.

LIBRA

He wasn't able to focus on just you. Libras have amazing social skills; they are beloved by everyone they meet. The problem arises when they can't turn this off, even when it becomes inappropriate and disrespectful to their partner. They may blame it on just having a way with people ("not their fault"), but you deserve someone who doesn't make you feel like you're in constant competition with everyone else they meet.

SCORPIO

He just wasn't a good person. The spark and intensity of Scorpio is irresistible at times, and you feel like you can tame them and get them to love you. But at the end of the day, they just aren't like other humans. They aren't loving, they aren't giving—they're constantly looking out for number one. You deserve someone who puts you first when you put them first, not to be in a relationship where you are both prioritizing the same person.

SAGITTARIUS

He couldn't take anything seriously. Sagittarians are great when you need a laugh or a lighthearted day. But if you are trying to be serious with Sagittarius in a maybe-I-want-you-to-be-my-life-partner kind of way, good luck. They're terminally chill and allergic to serious conversations, even though those are necessary for a healthy relationship. You deserve to date an adult and not a grown child.

CAPRICORN

He was cold. Capricorns are the ice kings of the zodiac. What little they do feel, they don't like to show. So, being in a relationship with Capricorn can be super unfulfilling. Unless you're equally unemotional, you're going to feel like you're in a relationship with a wall. You deserve to be in a relationship with someone who makes you feel loved—that's the whole point.

AQUARIUS

He couldn't be forthright about how he feels about you. Even though Aquarians tend to have gigantic hearts and care about being good people, they also like to be detached from others.

This means that while you are busy investing in them, they are investing in themselves. They don't want to show their cards or be too attached or run the risk of getting hurt. It's a coping mechanism of living life on the sidelines. You deserve someone who is all-in.

PISCES

He took your relationship for granted. Pisces think pretty highly of themselves in comparison to others. They think that because they don't *need* a relationship, they're somehow better than people who love to be in love. Because of this, they tend to take relationships for granted, assuming no one understands their deep, inner self. You deserve better than someone who thinks they are too smart and complex for your little tiny brain to fathom.

This Is How You're Going To Die (Probably)

BASED ON YOUR ZODIAC SIGN

ARIES

The most common last words for Aries are "hold my beer." Their adventurous spirit is an aspirational attribute until they do something gloriously stupid like riding a Segway off a cliff or disappearing while traveling to a foreign country they insist is "totally safe."

TAURUS

Taurus will die doing something they insist they can do alone, but shouldn't. Have fun being crushed underneath the bookshelf you thought you could move on your own!

GEMINI

Gemini will die by making friends with the wrong person. They're so friendly and positive that they see the good in everyone—even people that *scream* "bad for you." While they SWEAR they have excellent intuition, they'll die by their misplaced trust in a fixer-upper of a friend.

CANCER

Cancer will die of a broken heart or something equally sappy and lame. When something really bad happens, their self-destructive habits come out. They'll wallow until their resolve to keep going fizzles.

LEO

Leo will die in a desperate plea for attention. Every #selfiedeath has been a Leo.

VIRGO

Virgo will die at the office. On a holiday weekend.

LIBRA

Libra will die doing something for someone they love. There will be a flu-shot shortage one year and they'll forgo one out of the goodness of their hearts—and then get the flu and die.

SCORPIO

Scorpio will die in a fight with someone over a topic they've already forgotten about. They will leave instructions to make sure their obituary clarifies that they won.

SAGITTARIUS

Sagittarius will die of laughter, probably at their own joke.

CAPRICORN

Capricorn will die of old age on a deathbed, surrounded by all the people who have disappointed them in their lives so they can spend their last few hours being let down one last time.

AQUARIUS

Aquarius will die helping someone in need—at their own expense. They'll pick up a hitchhiker that plays on their sense of duty or get hurt while trying to rescue someone from an accident.

PISCES

Pisces will wander into traffic while writing a poem on their iPhone or getting lost in the lyrics to whatever dreamy song is playing in their headphones.

This Is How Your Partner Prefers To Say "I Love You"

BASED ON THEIR ZODIAC SIGN

♈ ARIES

Like Aladdin, Aries wants to show you the world. They care about adventure and about having an exciting life—by bringing you along, they are showing you they want you to be a part of this life. They demonstrate their love with actions, the acts of including you in their busy social calendars.

♉ TAURUS

Taurus in love does two things: They open up to you, and they feed you good food. It's pretty easy to tell where you stand with Taurus, because they don't play games. If you're in their inner circle, they are open and friendly; if you're not, they can be cold and closed-off. Pair this with their love of good food and you'll end up with an "I love you" that looks a lot like wining and dining (or just pizza and good sex).

♊ GEMINI

Geminis are notoriously flighty, so it can be intimidating to be in a relationship with them, wondering if they'll wake up tomorrow and feel just as strongly about some other guy or girl. But when they're in love, they like to make their passions all about the person they're in love with. They'll want to sign up for a cooking class together, learn to meditate together, or manufacture soaps to sell on Etsy—whatever it is, they make you part of it.

CANCER

Cancers *love* love, so if they love *you*, you'll know it. They'll say "I love you." They'll touch you. They'll make your favorite breakfast and bring it to you in bed. You will generally feel like you're a special person to them, and they are going out of their way to nurture you and show you that you are loved.

LEO

Leos are confident and charismatic, but in such a subtle way you might not immediately notice that this is true. When they're in love, they use these talents on their partner. Notice how your Leo acts around neutral people—like acquaintances or a customer-service person—and then notice how they act toward *you*. Leos say "I love you" with a charm that makes their partner realize how lucky they are.

VIRGO

Virgo won't say "I love you"—they'll just kind of hope you figure it out. What they will do is try to make your life better. They'd rather organize your parents' high-maintenance 50th-anniversary party than have a sappy word cross their lips. They care about you; they're just bad at expressing it with actual words.

LIBRA

When Libra is in love, they make you the center of their social circle. Gifted with people, this is the ultimate prize for Libra. You're their center of attention, the person they show off, and the one they come home to. They want everything in their social life to be harmonious—and all of it to revolve around the one they love.

SCORPIO

Scorpio says "I love you" by doing what they do best—fighting. They'll become extremely protective of you. Suddenly, someone insulting you is as bad as someone insulting *them,* and they're willing to take a stand to make it right.

SAGITTARIUS

Sagittarius says "I love you" by making you laugh. Having fun is one of their favorite things in the world, so they want *you* to experience it. They'll ham it up for you at every opportunity and make it their mission to keep a smile on your face.

CAPRICORN

It may sound counterproductive, but Capricorn will be pickier with someone they love than with someone they don't care about. Capricorns are particular individuals (but only because they know best), so when they love someone, they want that person to be the best that they can be. They'll push you toward career advancement, help you look your best when you go out together, and generally try to morph you into the most put-together version of yourself.

AQUARIUS

Aquarians love to understand the feelings of others, even if the ideas behind them seem alien. But they are selfless, even if they aren't mushy about saying it all the time. If they love you, your Aquarius will demonstrate how valuable you are by acts of service. They'll take your car to be serviced, walk your dog, install your Wi-Fi—it's a show-but-don't-tell method. They move slowly in love, but they'll get there.

PISCES

Like Cancers, Pisces revel in the *feeling* of being in love. Unlike Cancers, instead of focusing on the other person, they'll internalize the feeling and weave it into their inner life. If they're a writer, they'll fill diary pages with writing about you. If their craft is music, they'll write songs about you. They won't be knocking your door down for praise with what they've done, so you'll have to look closely and pay attention to when they use you as their muse.

Index

CHRISSY STOCKTON is a writer, thinker, and creative cheerleader based on the internet. She has a degree in philosophy and if she could have any superpower, she would be able to talk to dogs. Chrissy is the author of *Your Heart Will Heal: A Gentle Guided Journal for Getting Over Anyone*, *We Are All Just A Collection Of Cords*, a poetry collection, and creator of the essay compilation *What I Didn't Post On Instagram*. Follow her on Instagram @x.lane.s.